PUBLIC WELFARE
Notes from Underground

by
Michael Greenblatt
and
Steven S. Richmond

with Foreword by
Alexander E. Sharp

SCHENKMAN PUBLISHING COMPANY
CAMBRIDGE, MASSACHUSETTS

Copyright © 1979
Schenkman Publishing Company, Inc.
3 Mt. Auburn Place
Cambridge, MA 02138

Library of Congress Cataloging in Publication Data

Greenblatt, Michael.
  Public welfare, notes from underground.

  1. Social services — Massachusetts.
2. Social work administration — Massachusetts.
I. Richmond, Steven S., joint author.   II. Title.
HV98.M39G73   361.6'2'09744   79-3938
ISBN 0-87073-767-8
ISBN 0-87073-766-X pbk.

Printed in the United States of America

Preface

In *Public Welfare: Notes From Underground,* we select and explore some aspects involved in conducting social work. Our purpose is to provide readers with a coherent, faithful picture of the job. In order to give concrete accounts, we keep as near to social workers' actual job experiences as possible, and sometimes expand on our subject in places where we have special interests.

It is not our intention to explore the technical differences of each social worker's job title. For example, in the chapter on social services, the terms "family social worker," "child welfare social worker" and other specialized designations are treated as interchangeable terms. The targeted functions of these workers may be different, but the social work issues and experiences of each are generally alike.

In no way do we touch on all, or even most, of the facets open to authors writing on such a broad subject. For example, we do not *primarily* stress the financial aspects of welfare programs; many of these aspects are, however, contained in our Appendix. We do not expand on the regrettable and vulnerable condition of children in foster placement.* Our purpose is mainly to give the "flavor" of an increasingly important job.

Parts of this book can serve as a beginning and practical guide for conducting casework. A practical account of the social worker's job, we feel, is possibly the best way to present information to the general public as well as to provide learning materials to students of social work and public administration. We are especially concerned with setting our account against the larger backdrop of public human services across the country. Massachusetts is only one state, but it has earned a reputation as a leader in Welfare Administration. Our book, we hope, will cast a new

*For this, readers will find a valuable description in Alan R. Gruber's book, *Children in Foster Care* (Human Services Press, New York, 1978). For an indispensible discussion of the clinical and legal issues involved in child placement, readers will need to refer to *Beyond the Best Interests of the Child* by Joseph Goldstein, Anna Freud and Albert J. Solnit (Free Press, 1973).

light on how well Massachusetts is doing, though it may not bring about any sweeping changes in the delivery of Massachusetts' public services. Often we discuss large governmental and social questions in order to demonstrate how these contexts affect the thinking, morale and growth of social workers. We have chosen to be very personal and 'opinionated' in this book in order to best represent the *actual*, as opposed to the *theoretical*, conditions of our job.

Acknowledgements

We acknowledge with thanks the help given by the following individuals with whom we have worked and/or had lengthy and valuable discussions on the subject of social work: Thomas Luce, Robert Lapadula, David Aiken, Eloise Palumbo, Theo Stewart, Laurie Kobick, Ellen Patashnick, Stephen Babbitt, Cynthia Muir, Tony Luongo, Elena Powers, Frank Mihovan, Edna Goldsmith, Jean Connelly, Eileen Cooney, Alice MacDonald, Lila Kaufman, Anne Studley, Stella Raudenbush, Mike D'Entremont, Rick Kaplan, Lyn Shafer and Emma Evan.

In addition, we note our appreciation to the following organizations for the fine work they perform in the interest of children and families: DPW-Roxbury Crossing Social Service Units #100 and #200, Boston Juvenile Court, Children's Protective Services, Boston Children's Services Association, Family Services Association, DPW-Group Care Unit, DPW-Adoption Placement Unit, Massachusetts Adoption Resource Exchange, Crittendon-Hastings House, Suffolk County Probate Court, and the Massachusetts Mental Health Center.

No acknowledgement can be complete without recognizing the thousands of foster parents who open their homes to children in the Department's care. Foster parents represent one of the greatest human resources available to the Department. They are among the least rewarded.

Finally, we thank Beverly Uze Greenblatt and Martha E. Richmond for supporting and agonizing over this book.

Boston, Mass.   Michael Greenblatt
January, 1979   Steven S. Richmond

BIOGRAPHICAL SKETCHES

Michael Greenblatt is a Presidential Management Intern, currently employed by the Veterans Administration in Brockton, Massachusetts. From 1974 to 1977 he worked as an Assistance Payments Social Worker for the Department of Public Welfare in Boston, Massachusetts. From 1977 to 1978, he worked on a Medicaid project for the Department.

Mr. Greenblatt holds a B.A. in English from the University of Massachusetts and a Master's degree in Public Administration from Northeastern University.

* * *

Steven S. Richmond is a Senior Social Worker with the Department of Public Welfare-Group Care Unit in Boston, Massachusetts. He began working for the Department in 1973 as a Child Welfare Social Worker in Boston. In 1974, he worked for a brief period as an Assistance Payments Social Worker; and, beginning in 1975, he worked for two years as a Social Services Generalist Social Worker. He joined the Group Care Unit in 1977.

Mr. Richmond holds B.A. and M.A. degrees and is presently working toward a Master's degree in Public Administration at Suffolk University.

FOREWORD

Public Welfare: Notes from Underground is a valuable and useful book. This is so for exactly the reasons the authors thought that it would be valuable. Their assumption is that the world of the social worker ought to be set forth in concrete, very specific terms, and they want to share experience rather than theory. They succeed in their goal.

I do not know how prevalent is the myth of a social worker as being a pristine spinster or glazed functionary. Sterotypes will always exist. But what *is* surprising about the perception of social workers is that most people do not even approach an understanding of the profoundly good things social workers try to achieve and against what odds and obstacles. Mr. Richmond writes in this volume, without a trace of self-serving, "...it is the importance of the work which has kept the individual social worker going." How right he is! Social workers work out of offices that are, at best, dingy; they work for low pay, with telephones and typewriters that do not work; for people they frequently cannot help, in an often dangerous environment; and in a larger society which for the most part does not care. In all these ways, as well as others, workers are truly underground.

A cluster of books appeared in the late 1960's, several of them compelling, about what it is like to teach in inner city schools — Herbert Kohl's *36 Children* and Jonathan Kozol's *Death at an Early Age* among others. These books had the power of authenticity because they were written by people doing what they were writing about. There have, of course, been first-hand accounts from individuals in professions other than teaching. Dennis Smith was commercially successful with his *Report from Engine Company No. 82;* this described fire fighters in New York City. The appeal of this genre depends more on the sensitivity and verbal power of a writer than on a particular occupational arena. I would guess, for example, that narratives of a tax collector, a psychiatrist, a district attorney, and a minister would all have roughly equal chance at reaching an audience.

That having been said, however, there is extraordinary importance in the attempt of two social workers to convey their experiences on the front line. There have been remarkably few books, if any, which set forth — unfiltered — the hard life and, occasionally, the satisfaction of being a social worker. *Notes from Underground,* for instance, describes one case in which one of the authors had reason to believe that he would be physically attacked when he began his meetings with the client and was later harassed by phone calls in the middle of the night. In another case, he worked with a boy who was constantly running from foster homes; found himself at one point wrestling with the boy who had threatened him with a knife; located a home where it appeared that he might be able to grow; and, in the end, learned that he had been beaten to death by his step-brother. His last act on the case was to arrange for the funeral.

These brief sentences do not do justice to the narratives in the book. I mention them to point out that the extraordinary fact about them is that they are so ordinary in the lives of social workers. The families which the authors, and others, work with have already been shuttled around; their problems are too complex to be handled by any one agency; they suffer from a pathology of the poor (no single "solution" is likely to make much difference in their lives); and they have come to the Welfare Department because nobody else can help them.

As workers in the "agency of last resort" it is literally true that Department staff often are faced with letting a child wander the streets or taking him home for the weekend. Lack of resources does not help. In one instance, the Director of a Welfare Office lived for three days in a motel with a severely disturbed boy. The child had been placed there by a judge who wanted to dramatize the fact that the Department had no other facility which could keep the boy from running.

Social work must be described from the front lines for another reason. Few areas of social policy are more controversial than welfare. One reason welfare is such a difficult social issue is that there are no easy generalizations about why people are poor. There are deeply held views on whether people need help because they cannot help themselves or because they simply do not bother to try. Social workers are probably in a better position to comprehend these complexities than are representatives of most other professional groups. While the authors do not deal with these issues in any depth (nor did they intend to), they do describe the people who must be understood if these questions are ever to be answered.

I hope especially that this book will be read by legislators, because it is they, along with welfare administrators, who have the power to change some of the conditions described here. A Massachusetts state senator once said to me when we were discussing some budget hearings in which we had both participated in past years: "I sometimes think that my colleagues purposely don't give the Welfare Department what it needs, because if they did, it might function properly and they (the Legislature) wouldn't have anything to attack the Governor about." I do not think the Senator's statement (assuming he was serious, which he appeared to be) is an accurate one. But I do think that most legislators mirror their constituents in not knowing what welfare staff are trying to do and what they need to get it done.

Notes from Underground should be used as a teaching document in the classroom. I assume that somewhere along the line students in social work classes are shown Wiseman's film *Welfare,* which tells more about working in a welfare office than a stack of one hundred textbooks. In some ways, this book is the verbal analogue to the Wiseman film. Clearly it can be used to the same ends. It conveys feelings and experience rather than theory, and thereby communicates at an emotional level that most books do not even attempt.

Nor is its value limited to those who plan to be social workers. It can help administrators and legislators because it poses issues which are central to the operation of welfare agencies and, in some instances, to any large bureaucracy.

Mr. Greenblatt, in sections on The Welfare Office and on Assistance Payments, tells his personal story; it is not a pleasant one. He describes himself (and presumably many of his colleauges) as being victimized over a period of three years by the System, which he defines: too narrow a job; low salary; cockroach-infested offices; increased pressure from supervisors; computer printouts; a bad system for distributing workload; and program cutbacks. He describes a gradual erosion of the spirit and mentions tequila (as opposed to coffee) breaks and valium as antidotes to the dehumanization which he feels on the job.

I do not know the extent to which he is a victim of the System, as he portrays it, and how much should be attributed to his own psyche. I do know, however, that his depiction of life in the Department raises a question central to the administration of public welfare agencies. Will workers be motivated to do a good job when their primary responsibility is to determine the proper level of cash assistance for their clients, as compared to "merely" providing social services?

Few would disagree that computers should assist rather than hinder staff; that the number of cases per worker should be set at a reasonable level (to the extent that it is not); that the Department should have programs which meet the needs of people. But were these concerns answered, my guess is that many social workers would still disagree with the concept that certain workers ought to focus their efforts on assistance payments cases and others on providing social services. This is not a simple question; it begs, for example, the corollary question of how much of an assistance payments worker's time and energy should be directed to "soft" services — such as the search for adequate housing, budget counseling, and helping clients obtain other needed services. Should some workers be reduced, in other words, to being "eligibility clerks"; should they be nothing else?

Pivotal to all this is the question of how an agency decides to measure the performance of its staff. One of the most valuable aspects of Greenblatt's account is his describing the resentment which continually emerges over being asked to meet "quotas" by reviewing a specific number of cases. Until administrators began insisting on "quotas" there had been no measure by which to gauge the productivity of any worker within the Department. It seems essential to know the number of cases which are being handled by each staff member. But what this book makes clear, without specifically articulating the point, is that in measuring productivity, and in gathering information which will be used to determine how well staff are doing their job, it is essential to measure for the right things. If the goal is to determine whether workers are adequately determining the eligibility of cases, one must have a process for establishing not only how many cases they review each month but whether these redeterminations are accurate. Mr. Greenblatt had reason to be angry at a performance appraisal system which measured the amount of *"activity"* of a worker without seeking to gauge the *quality* of the work. It is possible, of course, to evaluate staff performance against this criterion, and such an approach is being implemented, at least in Massachusetts.

But assuming that the matter of "quotas" is put in perspective, the central question still remains: can staff obtain the satisfaction necessary to do a job well if their primary focus is on eligibility determination? The satisfaction persons feel in a job depends to a great degree on what they expect that job will be. The federal mandate to "separate" assistance payments from social services changed the nature of the work which many social workers had been trained for and wanted to perform. The emphasis on reducing the "error rate" (the percentage of cases which are not administered in conformity with federal regulations) is changing it even more. But this change, and the corresponding dissatisfaction, will not be felt to the same degree by those who join a Department with a clear sense of the assistance payments job as it is now defined. The error rate has been reduced over the last five years in Massachusetts, but is still significantly lower in some other states. I do not believe that assistance payments staff in these states feel as frustrated as this book implies even though the assistance payments job might be narrowly defined. If this is correct, much of the alienation Greenblatt describes may disappear.

Steven Richmond's thoughtful essay on Social Services raises the compelling question of when, if ever, it makes sense to subject an agency to significant reorganization. Separation of staff into either assistance payments or social services was accompanied in the specific case he discusses by much suffering; cases were shifted between workers, often breaking bonds of trust that had taken months if not years to establish. The Massachusetts Department can now anticipate yet another massive reorganization because of new legislation which moves the Office of Social Services out of the Department and reconstitutes it as a separate agency.

There is no question that reorganization very often solves little, creates problems, and deals with issues that could have been handled in other ways. The burden of proof is clearly on those who would reorganize. But there may be situations where reorganization *is* justified. Concerning the new agency, for example, I, as an administrator, was one who became convinced that the magnitude of the problems facing social services was so great that the only way to have a significant impact on them was to go through the process of creating a separate department.

The number of child abuse reports had increased over thirty-fold in six years, from 700 in 1974 to over 25,000 anticipated for

1979; there is a limit to which a bureaucracy can be overhauled without fundamental changes. Probably the most critical need is a review of all social services staff and reassignment of individual workers based on this evaluation. The prospects for this happening within the existing Massachusetts Department structure, absent the spotlight of outside attention which accompanies reorganization, were not promising. Nor did it seem that a piecemeal approach within the Department to problems of program planning, information systems, space, and civil service, could bring about change commensurate with the size of the issues to be addressed — certainly not within an acceptable amount of time.

Public Welfare: Notes from Underground raises many other important questions. What are the most effective ways of communicating to all levels of an agency consisting of over 100 local offices, and 5600 employees in six regional districts across a state? More specifically, what is the appropriate role, if any, of regional offices in such a structure? (They can easily become a bottleneck rather than transmitters of information.) To what extent should authority over matters such as budget planning, contracting with private agencies, and personnel administration be managed locally rather than out of one central office?

This book will help individuals to be better social workers and administrators. Less certain, of course, is the impact it will have on a broader audience and, as a consequence, on those who can provide agencies in all states with what is needed truly to meet the needs of the poor, the needs of troubled parents and kids. Mr. Richmond is not very optimistic on this score. He points out, again accurately, that society has never even come close to investing adequately in welfare services. As a result, social workers are always faced with trying to repair broken lives rather than figuring out how to keep them together. Maybe this will never change. If it does it will be because enough people have been told what the problems are, why they exist, and what is needed to deal with them. This is probably the most important reason why we should be grateful, no matter in what state we live, to these two authors for writing this book.

Alexander E. Sharp
Commissioner of Public Welfare
Commonwealth of Massachusetts
1976-1979

CONTENTS

CHAPTER ONE

THE WELFARE OFFICE: A CASE STUDY*

"No more would she (Ursula) subscribe . . . to the great machine
which has taken us all captives. In her soul, she was against it, she
disowned even its power. It had only to be forsaken to be inane,
meaningless. And she knew it was meaningless. But it needed a
great passionate effort of will on her part . . . still to maintain her
knowledge that it was meaningless."

* * *

"Her (Winifred's) real mistress was the machine . . . There,
there, in the machine, in the service of the machine, was she free
from the clog and degradation of human feeling. There . . . did
she achieve her consummation and her perfect union, her immor-
tality."

—D.H. Lawrence
The Rainbow

The Background

This case study describes the experience of an Assistance Payments Worker (also known as an Ongoing Worker or Social
Worker) in a local welfare service office in Boston.

Before 1968, the cities and towns of Massachusetts administered their own welfare programs. The system proved too
burdensome for some of the smaller, poorer towns. In an effort
to alleviate the burden, and to standardize welfare payments and
services to recipients, the state of Massachusetts took over the
administration of its welfare system in 1968.

*The following case study was published in a somewhat different version by the
Inter-University Case Program, Inc., Syracuse, N.Y., Edwin A. Bock, President.
The study is #121 in the I.C.P. series, Copyright © 1977, and is entitled *The
Welfare Office: Notes from The Underground* (by Michael Greenblatt).

The state was divided into regions, and each region had a number of local welfare service offices where recipients could be seen. Each social worker was assigned sixty cases; she was responsible for meeting all of the financial and many of the social service needs of her clients.

This system continued until September of 1974 when, under Federal mandate, services and financial management were separated into two distinct functions. As a consequence, workers were then assigned either to assistance payments (financial management) or to social service work.

One of the reasons for separation was the feeling that workers had too much to do, between determining financial eligibility and providing services. In addition, the Department was seeking to dispel a popular view that financial workers forced services upon their clients.

An opposing view, expressed by many experienced workers, held that the caseworker, in determining the financial needs of her client, was in the best position to determine her client's service needs.

Separation was not unique to Massachusetts. Other states had previously undergone some form of Separation, and there were a few accounts of the experience. One social worker in New Jersey told of how financial assistance workers and social service workers in her office became adversaries:

"The financial assistance workers tried to keep their clients away from the 'social work types' at all costs. The service workers would make a simple problem of a client not having enough money into a psychological case. The financial workers avoided their counterparts as often as possible."

Although stories like this one were heard, most workers did not know what to expect in the months ahead, after services and financial management were separated.

This case study concerns the largest welfare service office in the Boston Region. It is one of eleven local offices in the Region. At the time of this study, the office was one of the more tightly administered and better organized offices in the Region.

Forty-four Assistance Payments Workers were divided into eight units, with one supervisor in each unit. The average age of the workers was about twenty-eight.

In 1973, a prospective employee of the Department of Public Welfare had to take and pass a civil service examination in order to qualify for a position as an Assistance Payments Worker. In order to take the exam, one had to have earned a bachelor's degree in any subject.

In 1974, another examination was given. Eligibility for taking this exam included holding a bachelor's degree in any subject *or* having at least three years of paid professional or technical experience in a social service agency or program. Applicants were hired according to their marks on the exam with those scoring highest being the first to receive requisitions. (People who took the 1974 exam were just being contacted about openings in 1977.)

The 1974 exam concentrated more on personal attitudes than on expertise in the social work field. For example, applicants were graded on the basis of such questions as "Would you rather be an actor in or the director of a play?"

The starting salary for an Assistance Payments Caseworker in 1974 was $172.50 per week. In July of 1977, the social workers' Union negotiated a new contract in which the starting salary would be $188, beginning August 1st, 1977. (By comparison, the production worker in New England factories averaged $211.00 a week in October 1977, while Boston factory workers averaged $232.76 a week.)* However, some members of the State Legislature attached a rider to the State employees' pay raise bill. The pay raise could not be passed without passage at the same time of a controversial abortion bill, designed to prohibit the use of public monies for most abortions. In November of 1977, the Governor line-item vetoed the abortion bill, the raise was approved, and workers received their August increase in their December paychecks.

A local of the State Employees' Union represents welfare case workers, supervisors, and clerical staff. (As of 1978, workers had to belong to the Union and pay dues of $2.50 a week.) Workers had not won a Union contract until they struck for and gained one in 1969.

---

*Secretaries in Boston averaged $203.00; in Dallas, $196.00; in Indianapolis, $209.00; in Los Angeles, $229.00; in Miami, $197.50; in Buffalo, $206.50.[1]

The Story

When I came to the Department of Public Welfare in September of 1974, the Department had just begun its administrative split into two main areas — financial assistance and social services. With the 1974 division, each financial social worker was assigned 120 cases, double the previous caseload. The Union contract showed that each worker could be assigned up to 180 cases.

I began as an Assistance Payments Worker. When I started work in September, my caseload was assigned on the basis of area. I was assigned cases according to certain streets, and I came up with the Bromley-Heath Projects, one of the most troubled housing projects in Boston. Assignment by area allowed each worker to get a feeling for a specific neighborhood and its special problems, and travel was made easier, since a worker could visit different people in the same locality.

During the first few months, everything was quite confused due to the new separation of roles in our office. Nobody was quite sure what his function was, and clients were still accustomed to having one social worker for all of their needs. Before, the workers were accustomed to providing social services, and many continued to do so although they quickly noticed a strain due to their increased caseloads.

The unit in which I began my work was made up of seven workers. We had no supervisor; this presented no hardship most of the time. The people in my unit were knowledgeable; they helped me with policy interpretation and other questions. Three had been with the Department for more than five years. Three were working for advanced degrees and planned to leave when they received them.

We were a fairly "client-oriented" unit, which meant that we often tried to interpret Department policy in favor of the clients. At that time, there was adequate flexibility for us to use our discretion on many issues; and many issues arose each day. For example: The first few months I was there, I encountered the policy known as Emergency Assistance. Clients who were in emergency need of furniture and appliances could secure them with funds from the Department. The worker had to visit each client's home to decide if the need existed.

The availability of Emergency Assistance became known to clients by word of mouth, and requests began to pour in. We processed a good number of these requests after visiting many homes and observing much decrepit furniture. Any number of examples could be given. One woman had no crib for her infant, who had to sleep in the top drawer of a bureau. Another woman's household furniture consisted of torn plastic beach chairs; she kept her milk in a small styrofoam chest because she had no refrigerator.

One client manipulated her E.A. benefits to move to Florida. For months, she had told her worker how she hated living in the housing projects. She wanted to move but said that she had little money. Nothing could be done for her. One day, she came in to request E.A. for new furniture. The worker visited the client's home and found the furniture in disrepair. The papers were processed, and the furniture was delivered. A few weeks later the client came to the office and told her worker that someone had broken into her apartment and had stolen the $900 that she had saved to move to Florida. Again, nothing could be done for her. Not long after, the worker was informed by a friend of the client, that the client had sold the new furniture and had used the money to move south.

The E.A. program involved substantial paperwork and mathematical figuring. Apart from receiving large furniture items, clients were allowed certain small household goods. For example, the Department allowed three facecloths per person, at 67¢ each. Towels, sheets, blankets, as well as clothing were similarly matched to allowable costs. The workers would sit at their desks, multiplying all day long — so many people, so many facecloths, times 67¢. For workers this was simply added to their routine case maintenance responsibilities, to be performed under increased work pressures.

Once the worker processed the E.A. applications, there were often long delays in delivery of the goods. The paperwork had to be checked and signed by a supervisor, then by a head administrator, and then sent to the regional office for final approval. Calls would come in constantly about the delays.

When furniture was finally delivered, some tables arrived with only three legs. Some washers were of a smaller capacity than had been promised by the salesclerk. Other items were simply not what had been ordered. At this time many workers felt as if they were working in the complaint department of the local furniture store. In addition, payments to store owners were delayed and the stores began to hound the workers for their money.

The E.A. Program came into controversy. It soon became apparent that the Department was spending a lot of money on the Program. Emergency Assistance appealed to some workers because it met their clients' needs and allowed them to exercise personal judgment in their clients' behalf. Some workers thought it was a give-away program. Others resented their clients' ability to obtain new furniture. Still others were angry with the enormous amount of paperwork involved in processing requests. Many workers and administrators were disturbed because E.A. policy guidelines were so flexible. Clients welcomed the opportunity to purchase new or replace worn furniture.

Administrators and workers argued over the Program. It was felt that some workers were processing too many furniture requests. I, for instance, was told to spend more of my time in investigative work and less time on Emergency Assistance applications.

One administrator accused a worker of lying about his clients' needs in an effort to slow up some of the workers' requests. One morning the worker entered the administrator's office to see if one of his E.A. requests had been signed. He located the case record; on top of it was a note written by this administrator to another administrator. It read: "I am tired of this guy. I don't believe the date of receipt of estimate. What do you think?" The worker, realizing that this note challenged his integrity and would have the effect of delaying the E.A. request, as well as others he would submit on behalf of his clients, asked for a meeting with this administrator.

In the meeting, at which the worker and his union representative were present, the administrator explained that the word "guy" referred to the *forms*, not to the worker, and that the administrator was tired of processing the forms and not tired of the worker. The worker found this explanation unacceptable and filed a Union grievance, citing the administrator's unprofessional behavior as one of the reasons for the grievance. The grievance remained unresolved for over a month; it was eventually dismissed by the Department with the suggestion that the administrator thereafter approach similar situations in a different manner.

Approximately six months from the time I encountered the Emergency Assistance Program, it was revised. It was costing the state too much money.

Increased Caseloads and Redetermination Quotas

During these early months, a few members of my unit and I took walks during our coffee breaks. We walked for about fifteen minutes, talked, and then returned. We also lunched together frequently, and we organized a few parties on different occasions. We communicated freely in the office and discussed ways to approach the job and to help clients; in general, there was a good amount of laughter and spirit.

About four months into the job, January 1975, the workers' caseloads were increased from 120 to 160-180 cases. Workers refused to handle this number of cases, feeling that they could not cover all of them adequately. The excess cases, that is, forty to sixty per worker, were left uncovered, or "dumped," until the Department went to court to enforce the Union contract, which documented 180 as the maximum case load. As a result, administrators had to see those clients whose cases were dumped. Resentment and tension between workers and administrators followed. Workers were glad that administrators got a taste of the front line. The court finally ordered workers to carry their contractual 180 cases. People resumed their appointed roles once again. But some people held grudges.

A typical assignment of 180 cases consisted of 479 people.[2] The worker on this caseload was responsible for overseeing monthly budgets totaling $46,641.50, not including food stamp payments.

Workers began to worry that these caseload increases were a prelude to a switch from *case*loads to *work*loads. Under a workload system, workers do not have any assigned, regular clients; rather, they see people on a rotational basis as they come into the office.

The workload system was in effect in New York City, and those in our office familiar with it dreaded this system. It was reported to be a beserk experience, confusing, frustrating and totally dehumanizing. However, as the months passed, our caseload system remained.

At this time, the Department began to stress another work task mentioned in the contractual agreement: the "redetermination quota." Redeterminations are six-page forms which contain a series of investigative questions to be answered by each client. The questions are about the client's children, finances, health, etc. Under the Union contract, a worker with 120 cases had to complete twenty-five redeterminations per month. Some time later, the quota was increased to forty redeterminations for 120 cases.

The following summarizes the Department's administrative policies and procedures affecting financial assistance redeterminations.

Massachusetts is reimbursed by the Federal Government for the money it pays to welfare recipients under the A.F.D.C. Program (Aid to Families with Dependent Children). Reimbursement runs from 50% to 75%, depending on the nature of the payment to the recipient. In order to receive the maximum amount, states in this Program must have a low error rate in their cases.

Federal auditors visit offices to check samples of cases, and if the error rate exceeds the official rate allowed, a state may lose its reimbursement. Examples of errors in cases are underpayments or overpayments to a client, the absence of a required form in the case record, or an incorrect determination of eligibility.

If a state has a high error rate, it must submit a corrective action report to the Federal Government, stating how it intends to lower errors within a certain time period.

Case errors are a larger problem than most people realize. Welfare fraud is usually considered the 'number one' drain on the system. A recent government study conducted, in part, on H.E.W.'s A.F.D.C. Program reveals otherwise. The study found that the Program loses about 1 billion dollars a year from fraud. The loss from case errors is 6.4 billion dollars. Despite these lop-sided figures, officials continue to concentrate more heavily on fraud, partly because of its sensational, emotional nature. The problem becomes more magnified, considering that there are only two budgets on earth larger than that of the Department of H.E.W., these being the budgets of the United States and the Soviet Union.

Redeterminations are seen as a major administrative tool for keeping error rates low. The Federal Government requires that six-page redetermination forms, which may involve up to forty pages of additional forms before they are complete, be filled out twice a year by each client and her caseworker. The Massachusetts Legislature has mandated that they be filled out three times a year by each client, but this is not carried out.

To the client, the redetermination form means that every six months she must come into the office with certain required papers: a rent receipt, bank statements, and wage stubs if she works. Other papers are required under varying circumstances. There is a question on the form that asks the client if she works. The client may respond yes or no, and if the response is no, that is as far as it goes.

Most clients come in, answer the questions asked, sign the form at the bottom, and leave. It is an obligation every six months, but quickly over and forgotten for most. Some clients have a hard time delivering the required papers, and they must constantly be badgered. Often they resent the whole process.

For the agency, redeterminations are an effective way to keep the error rate down and satisfy Federal guidelines. The quotas impose pressures on caseworkers to see a certain number of clients a month: the Department feels that this is necessary to prevent errors.

For workers, redeterminations mean meeting quotas and filling in endless forms that many think are meaningless and useless. Redeterminations are considered to be unrealistic, inappropriate indicators of worker performance, and their effect on the error rate is greatly exaggerated. This is because redeterminations are carried out in a system where:

1) the client is the primary source of information: this leads to inaccurate and delayed information because

   a) Department oversights (such as computer mistakes or unclear policies) cause clients difficulty in providing the proper information,

   b) worker ignorance of the Manual causes clients to be misinformed, which causes them difficulty in providing the proper information, and

   c) clients, either deliberately or unintentionally, fail to provide the proper information:

2) workers carry 180 cases, a fact which is responsible for many oversights, and

3) many of the required forms serve no other purpose than to add paper to case records.

When the Department began to stress redetermination quotas, our entire office staff talked in terms of redeterminations. This became the main focus of the job; we were judged on the number of forms that we completed. A graph which displayed the division of the office into units was hung on the second floor wall. It showed the number of redeterminations each unit had completed. The graph was torn down the day after its appearance. The next day, the office administrators put another sign in its place stating: "We know who tore down the sign."

In February 1975, our unit received a full-time supervisor. During the month, one worker in our unit — the one who had been called a liar — was asked to submit an advance schedule of his activities during the day, because his redeterminations were very low. (Workers have a 9 to 5 day, but we are allowed to "go into the field;" originally this was to visit with people in their homes, but now it was only for purposes of redeterminations.)

The worker "grieved" (i.e., initiated a grievance complaint under Union procedures) this advance scheduling on the grounds of discrimination, since others with low redeterminations had not been singled out. After a few months, the advance scheduling order was dropped.

We all went on for a few months with each of us servicing 160-180 cases.

Many clients were Spanish-speaking people who had great trouble understanding and filling out forms, at the same time the entire office had only three Spanish-speaking employees. As the number of cases increased, the interviewing space in the office decreased, and clients were questioned in hallways. Workers often grabbed bi-lingual clients from the waiting area to interpret for their Spanish cases, so that people often had to relate — to total strangers — information about their private affairs. Case workers felt less and less professional, and client confidentiality was being destroyed. A Union grievance was filed, but no action was taken.

Interviewing space was not the only physical problem in the building. Although the janitors tried their best, many of the cramped rooms — walls, floors, windows — were dirty. Ventilation was poor in the summer. On muggy summer days the inside air was still and oppressive.

Cockroaches, a city-wide problem, were a source of special irritation at work. One worker suggested unrolling cuffed pants after visiting the bathroom, to make sure that roaches would not be taken home. Sometimes, though, roach eggs were laid on workers' clothing and in their purses. A few workers had brought these eggs home and had to fumigate their houses. Another worker, agitated by the bug problem, placed a large roach in an envelope and sent it to the Welfare Commissioner. However, the Commissioner's secretary was the first to open the envelope, and she bore the brunt of the complaint.

A few workers painted their rooms, one or two even carpeted and furnished them. These rooms were bright and clean. But, in general, the surroundings were dismal.

Our unit now had less time for conversation relating to clients or otherwise. Paper began to generate more paper, and we all felt the strain of increased caseloads. Assistance Payments Workers began to sense the hopelessness of trying to serve the clients' social service needs as they had done before. We were now forced by our higher caseloads to refer most service needs to the service units. Even so, many of our referrals were held up because of a lack of direction or policy in the Social Service units, the system being so new. The clients still called us for help with their family problems.

In May of 1975, some CETA* workers joined our staff, so our caseloads returned to about 130 cases. However, workers began to quit the Department and absenteeism increased greatly. Also, workers began to "go into the field" in the afternoon to escape, rather than to work.

They slammed down phones quite frequently and "blew up" in the office. The phones were constantly ringing, grating upon everyone's nerves. Workers began to take tranquilizers frequently. Five milligrams of Valium was the dosage commonly used. Some workers withdrew to the roof and smoked marijuana, but returned to discover themselves even more jittery.

With the emphasis on redetermination quotas, clients came to be seen as numbers to be compiled against work quotas. Less complicated cases, requiring less paperwork, were viewed as good ones by some workers, while the sick or dysfunctional persons who never brought in the correct verifications were viewed as nuisances, as a hinderance to doing the job.

Budget Uncertainties

In June of 1975, state politics, the recession, and financial cutbacks began to be felt throughout the Department of Public Welfare. First, the Governor and the Legislature could not decide on a supplemental budget (the original budget was exhausted). So clients began to receive their checks late, while factions within the Government argued. More than once, workers and clients alike were threatened with payless weeks. Only at the last moment, on Friday afternoons, were the workers paid. The threats of payless weeks and impending lay-offs were with us through June and July. Clients were angered since they were not receiving their checks on time; one week, clients' checks were suspended for four days.

Then the Governor cut out a 5% cost of living increase for clients and workers. We were supposed to feel lucky just to be receiving a paycheck every week.

It was summer, 1975. Clients would have to wait over a year for their cost-of-living increases.[3] Workers had not received a pay raise since early in 1974 and would have to wait for one until

*Comprehensive Employment and Training Act.

autumn of 1976. In July of 1976 they struck for three days over a one-year contract; they finally won an average increase of $500.

Between October 1975 and October 1976, retail prices in Boston rose 6.9% (U.S., 5.3%). Between October 1976 and October 1977, Boston retail prices again rose 5.5% (U.S., 6.5%). Housing costs in Boston during 1976-77 gained 5.9%. Fuel oil and coal were up 12.2%, gas and electricity up 8.3%. Number 2 fuel oil, used in home heating, rose about $6.00, to $48.27 per 100 gallons.*

In the autumn of 1976, Boston was found to have the highest total budget costs for a family of four at the intermediate level, among 38 continental U.S. areas studied. The total annual cost of the autumn 1976 intermediate budget in Boston was $19,384, compared to a U.S. metropolitan average of $16,596.[4]

Meanwhile, workers took the calls of clients who simply could not adjust to their checks being delayed. They received some very abusive calls at this time from some justifiably angry clients. Their calls, however, were misdirected. It was not *our* fault. They blamed us anyway.

Finally, an interim budget was passed, but the Governor warned of future cuts. At this time, also, it was becoming very difficult to interpret Department policy in deciding benefits for clients, because policy was constantly changing, and because numerous cuts had begun to become effective. Many clients shouted at workers for promising benefits during one week which they could not deliver the next.

In all of this confused and frustrating time, the Department lent no supports to its workers, nor did administrators appear to care about the psychological damage being done to their staff members. The workers themselves were overwrought, many thought of quitting, and most considered themselves as being treated like lackeys by the Department. They had been hired as professionals, yet many of them expressed the thought, "They treat us the way they treat clients."

There were now only two of us going on walks during our morning coffee breaks. Many mornings, the Director of the building stood at his office window and watched the front door to make sure that everyone was in at exactly 8:45 a.m. Conversation in the office now centered mainly upon complaints about the job.

*Other sample examples: Food was up 5.6%. A pound of chicken was 8¢ higher, to 72¢ a pound. A pound of cream-filled cookies was up 20¢, to $1.20. Apparel rose 3.9%, public transportation 2.1%, private transportation 6.1%. Gasoline was 3¢ more per gallon, to $.621. Medical care was up 7.8%, personal care 4.9%, and reading and recreation 2.3%.

*Loss of Discretion
and Mounting Pressures*

As the winter of 1975-76 approached, most workers felt their jobs changing. The Department's program management people downtown who were devising special projects for the computer, had begun to eliminate all worker discretion on the job.

We received more and more computer print-outs. One month the computer misprinted a huge volume of Medicaid cards, leaving out children's names. At the bottom of each card, a statement read: "Contact your social worker in case of error." So the calls poured in, and the process of social workers becoming computer error correctors was underway.

More cuts were instituted in late 1975. Clients were put on *consolidated* grants, which cut out many special needs that had been previously included in the recipients' budgets. We were responsible for changing our caseloads from the old to the new grants while continuing our other work and explaining the new grants to our clients.

One Wednesday, just before we began the conversion process to the consolidated grant system, some workers received letters stating that they might be jobless by Friday due to budget constraints. On Friday, money in the State budget was switched from one account to another, and the workers were not laid off. We were given a ten-day deadline to complete the conversion process.

More administrative pressure came to many of us through letters reprimanding us for not meeting our redetermination quotas. There were three types of letters: not so bad, bad, and you are in for immediate administrative action. Which of the three letters we received depended upon the percentage of the quotas that we had fulfilled.

Another nagging problem was food stamps. People receiving welfare payments are entitled to receive food stamps. The Food Stamp Program is Federal, but the State Welfare Department administers it at the local office level. This means that social workers establish and monitor food stamp cases and make all necessary adjustments (including openings and closings) for their clients. In many months, recipients did not receive their food stamps, and we had to track them down. The food stamp office in our regional office downtown had only two telephone extensions. It often took days to get through. Then the Department decided that each time a redetermination was completed, a new food stamp application had to be taken. Two more pieces of paper were added to the pile.

Also, many of the Spanish-speaking clients thought they should be getting more food stamps. They could not understand the allotment system, which had to be explained to them through an interpreter.

Cutting the General
Relief Recipients and
Increasing Computer Projects

In November, 18,000 General Relief recipients (single adults, capable of work) would be cut from the State rolls. They would also be cut from Medicaid, except for life-sustaining drugs. One woman came to us at the office with no teeth. Her false teeth had been in her pocketbook, and her pocketbook had been stolen. Under present circumstances she could no longer purchase false teeth. As I sat and listened to her story, I wondered if I should do a redetermination on her in order to help meet my quota.

Most General Relief recipients did not call the office until they had not received their checks and finally realized that they had been denied assistance. They called and were told that they could appeal the decision and, once again, we had to grope for answers to the perennial question: "How will we live?"

The number of people who called was surprisingly low. However, those who did call were angry with the workers. After a few calls, the clients' complaints sounded the same. The workers had many other things to do, morale was at a low point and, consequently, complaints were handled poorly:

> *G.R.:* "I didn't get my check. Now what am I supposed to do? Do you want me to steal? Is that what you're saying to me? Go out and rip someone off? Is that what you want me to do? Bust someone over the head? Is that what you're telling me?"
> *Worker:* "Do what you want."

And the worker would hang up.

Other G.R. recipients who continued to be eligible were classified as unemployable due to disability. They had to be redetermined every six months, which meant that they had to present a medical report stating that they were disabled due to drug addiction, alcoholism, or some other problem. As soon as they could perform regular work, they would be cut off.

Some workers avoided redetermining these G.R. recipients since many of them were only partially recovered from disability and could not possibly hope to compete in the job market. If we cut them off, we cared about what would happen to them. These recipients made up almost one-third of our caseloads. Sometimes we had to get tough and close cases that were on the borderline in order to meet our quotas.

The Office of Research and Planning in the Department instituted a study in January 1976 "to assess the effects of termination of assistance and medical coverage on G.R. recipients." When they had trouble getting responses from former recipients, they sent us the questionnaires and asked if we could locate former clients and help them fill out the forms. In addition, we were to remind clients that they would be eligible to receive $7.50 each for a response.

At this time, we were told that the State had begun use of a computer which could detect duplicate names and social security numbers and could be used to discover recipients who were collecting benefits in more than one state. More and more computer projects were being passed on to us. One computer print-out came to us with a list of clients who had reported post office boxes instead of street addresses. We had to contact all of our clients by a certain date to verify that they had a permanent address.

Apart from computer specialists, people from Quality Control, the unit that checks errors in the cases, would call and tell us to close those cases in which the client had not come in for a scheduled interview with the Quality Control representative. Often, a case would be closed upon demand, only to have the client come in a few days later, angry with her social worker for closing it.

A special person in the office worked on a computer print-out, seeking to find our clients among those on a list of clients receiving unemployment compensation. He gave us the names of the people who were collecting, and we had to call them in to close out or reduce their assistance. One print-out contained the names of people to whom the Department had sent letters but whose letters had been returned to us; we were ordered to close the cases. When we sent out routine letters and they were returned, addressee unknown, we were ordered to close these cases also. Many times, mail was returned in error, clients came in angry, and we had to re-open the case, a process requiring a ten-page re-application form.

In some instances the people downtown closed some cases in error, and we were responsible for straightening out the messes. We were becoming computer correctors. Incompetence correctors. Machines. (An interesting sidelight to all of this computer technology and takeover of our jobs was the practice of "scapegoating the computer.")

When a client did not receive a check on the correct date (clients receive checks on two days of the month, according to the last digit of their social security numbers), or if she was expecting a special payment and did not receive it, we had to call downtown and ask one of the computer clerks what happened. A clerk would often say that the information had not yet been fed into the computer. If we called back later the same day, another clerk would tell us that it had gone in yesterday. It was very hard to get a straight answer, and we were left to advise the client of a computer delay. Blame it on the computer.

Closing the Escapes

In January of 1976, more workers began to resign, and others were constantly taking sick days. Workers began to be called into the administrators' offices to give reasons for not reaching their quotas.

Naturally, some units had completed more redeterminations than others. The main reason for this was that there were different standards in each unit for what constituted a completed redetermination. Some supervisors demanded much more paperwork and verification than did others.

Sometimes, a supervisor would not count a redetermination unless the rent receipt was on an official rent receipt form. She would not accept a receipt on a plain piece of paper. Other supervisors let things go and accepted everything. One supervisor came out with a detailed description of what papers should be included in a completed redetermination, but this did nothing.

Workers were being pressured and judged on the basis of unequal standards, yet the workers only complained to each other. They tried to cope with the conflict in their own ways, keeping to themselves.

The job still had its escapes. One escape was, as I mentioned before, to leave the office early, to go into the field. Some workers went home after reporting on their time sheets that they had gone to visit a few clients to do redeterminations. These workers first made certain those same clients would come into the office the next morning for redeterminations. The administration knew of this practice, but allowed it to continue.

The quota system led workers into other forms of behavior. Some workers forged signatures and made up their own redeterminations when all of the required information was already in the records.

Due to workers leaving so rapidly and due to subsequent shuffling of cases, workers often inherited cases from other workers which had recently been redetermined. If all of the information had been obtained by the last worker and if it was in the record, the new worker would sometimes rip up the recent redetermination. He would then call in the client, saying that a mistake had been made, and she would sign another redetermination form. The worker would then complete and receive credit for an easy redetermination. Usually, the more complicated cases (the cases likely to contain the most errors), or the cases with special problems, were left for last. After all, the Department cared about compiling numbers; workers found ways to comply.

Around February of 1976, some workers were informed that they might lose their jobs because they had not taken the 1974 Civil Service exam for social workers. The Union took up the matter, and it was later resolved.

Alphabetization,
Redistribution,
Frustration

Around this time, the administration decided that caseloads would be redistributed according to the alphabet so that everyone and everything would be more easily accounted for. We were to receive new clients whose last names began with letters from a section of the alphabet. First, we had to write down the names of all of our clients and their Social Security numbers. This information was to be fed into the computer. We balked at this, saying that it was an unreasonable addition to our work, for which there would be no compensation. The administration threatened suspensions, and the Union did nothing positive, so we completed the forms.

By this time, so many employees had left their jobs that the units were unequal in the numbers of their workers. The Department refused to hire new workers. One unit was staffed by two workers to cover a minimum of at least 600 cases. Neighboring service units had child abuse cases piling up on empty desks.

A month after first redistributing cases, another redistribution had to take place to equalize the units. Again we filled out the forms, recording information on all of our cases. Some cases were left with budgets only partially calculated; there was no sense of continuity of service in these caseloads. Many clients had no idea who their social workers were from one week to the next.

In April of 1976, we were informed that the Office of Research and Planning would do a study. Their study required us to fill out a form for every release that we sent to the computer during the month of May. The workers refused and were informed that they would be suspended for three days. Suspension letters were sent to about 600 workers and supervisors informing them of the impending suspensions and of the fact that a copy of the suspension letter would be placed in their personnel files.

The Union held a meeting and its spokesmen said that the Union would ask the Department for a reduction in redeterminations for the period in which the workers would participate in the study. The workers agreed and began filling out the forms. The Department went to court to seek enforcement of its orders. The court found in favor of administration. We were not granted any reduction in our redetermination quotas and the study was extended to June 18, 1976 to make up for the two weeks when we had refused to complete the forms.

At the end of May, the Director of our office said that he wanted anyone who had not completed 90% of his quota to return from the field to the office regularly at 4 p.m. (This policy has not yet become official. The Union is considering whether or not it is in violation of the workers' contract.) Also, letters were sent out to workers stating that, since they had not met their May quotas, they would have to meet every week with their supervisors and discuss techniques for improving their performance. If they could not meet 90% of their quotas, some necessary administrative action would follow.

One week, we received two computer print-outs. One print-out showed that the computer had mis-paid some of our clients, and we had to correct the mistake. Using the other print-out, we would be responsible for securing the alien registration numbers of certain Cuban refugees. Three more workers left during this month. All of these computer projects carried specific deadline dates, usually a few days from the date of receipt by the local office. Most of the demands from downtown carried the words, "priority redeterminations."

Downtown does not really care. This is where they want our jobs to end, the less worker discretion and client contact the better. The more mechanical the worker, the better.

FOOTNOTES
CHAPTER ONE

[1]Occupational Earnings and Wage Trends in Metropolitan Areas, 1977, Summary 78-5, U.S. Department of Labor, Bureau of Labor Statistics.

[2]Based on August 1978 statistics, 496,330 people were on some form of welfare in the state of Massachusetts, including A.F.D.C., G.R., Cuban and Vietnamese and Cambodian Refugee programs, and people who were only receiving Medicaid benefits. (The number of *people* is down from the previous year, while the number of *cases* has risen; thus there are more *families* receiving welfare this year than last). There were another 130,541 people on S.S.I., the Federal aged and disabled program (based on March 1978 statistics) (Department of Research and Planning, Massachusetts Welfare Department). There are approximately 5,789,480 people living in the State (figure as of March 1, 1975, Massachusetts Census Bureau). Also, based on a 1% sample, in a study done in the summer of 1975, the A.F.D.C. recipients are: 72.9% white; 15.4% black, non-Hispanic; 7.2% Hispanic, and 4.5% others (Massachusetts Welfare Department, Department of Research and Planning).

In a typical caseload: 1) The average age of the G.R.s is forty-two, 2) The average age of the A.F.D.C. parent is thirty-two, 3) The average family size is three people ($304.30 per month budget), 4) Seventy-one of the 130 A.F.D.C. families have children under six, which means that these women are exempt from the Work Incentive Program, 5) Twelve of the 130 A.F.D.C. clients report that they are working and, consequently, have deductions taken from their budgets, and 6) There are two unemployed fathers in the caseload.

[3]Again, in 1978, payment of a 6 percent July 1 cost-of-living increase for the 380,000 people on the state's A.F.D.C. program was delayed because restrictive language was written into the budget by the Legislature. As of the date of this writing, it appears that the cost-of-living raise could be delayed until the Legislature reconvenes January 1979 — even though the U.S. Department of Health, Education and Welfare has "told the state" that the restrictive language violates both the Social Security Act and H.E.W. regulations.

[4]Based on the Bureau of Labor Statistics Urban Family Budget Study, Autumn, 1976. Statistics in preceding paragraph and the Urban Family Budget Study were included in Regional Report Number 78-1, U.S.Department of Labor, Bureau of Labor Statistics, New England Regional Office.

CHAPTER TWO

ASSISTANCE PAYMENTS

"And what makes you so cocksure, so positive that only the normal and the positive, that is, only what promotes man's welfare, is to his advantage? Can't reason also be wrong about what's an advantage? Why can't man like things other than his well-being? Maybe he likes suffering just as much. Maybe suffering is just as much to his advantage as well-being. In fact, man adores suffering. Passionately. It's a fact."

—Dostoyevsky
Notes From Underground

I

The doors to our local welfare office open at 8:45 a.m. In good weather, there is often a small crowd of people, standing and sitting on the front steps, waiting to be admitted. At the side of the building, a door is opened for employees. A few workers use this entrance to avoid the crowded lobby, to secure a few moments of peace, important times to safeguard in an occupation filled with disturbance and commotion.

The worker trudges up the side stairs. The stairwell is dim and smells slightly musty. The walls are dull green. In places, the paint has peeled down from the walls but remains attached to it, like petrified pieces of torn wallpaper. The worker reaches his landing. He turns right and continues down the corridor to his second floor office: a small, dull, green room. There is a thin layer of grime on the floor and radiators, and dust balls in the corners. The room is meant for five workers.

Five bulky, gray metal desks are crowded into the room. Two desks face each other on one side of the room, three face the walls on the other side. There is a large window at the back. Warm sunlight will stream through in the afternoon, brightening the gray, metallic surroundings.

Downstairs, people form a line approaching the front desk. When it is their turn, they will give the clerk their name: if they are already receiving welfare, the clerk will call their worker on the phone, and the worker will eventually come down.

These people are familiar with the office routine, so they sit on a bench in the main lobby and wait. A few cause a commotion because they are drunk. In the waiting room just off the lobby, a woman sits and counts on her fingers, convincing herself that the figures she has tallied will get her through the month.

The waiting room has no furniture except for worn metal chairs placed against the walls. One woman leaves her chair to adjust the thermostat on one of the walls. It is the only thermostat in the building, so the temperature of every room will be regulated by the woman in this room.

II

I am a passive man. Events filter slowly through my system. I am no good in emergencies. I stand there with a dumb, quizzical stare while people bleed to death. My reactions are halting and studied. By studied, I do not mean a process of calculated thought. I mean that my *emotions* study the situation, and when certain feelings are stimulated, I begin to plod ahead.

To be sure, I can be as impulsive as the next person, running here or there for some small, seemingly important purpose. I can even make quick, intelligent decisions based on lucky guesses. But when something really big happens to me, such as being treated like an insect, I sit and stew. Finally, I will act, more out of whim than anything else. I would prefer not to act at all. I might just as well be one of the dull silver spheres in a pinball machine.

III

Early this morning, I was deciding how to change jobs. I had tried to go outside the Department, but no one would have me. Interviewers had treated me rudely, and they never called back when they said they would. I did not seem qualified for any of the positions.

My resulting decision was to look for another job within the Department, anything to get away from Assistance Payments. Two and a half years was enough. I had settled on "Intake," after talking to a few workers in that section.

Intake Workers interviewed welfare applicants and filled out the necessary application forms with them. They saw about eight or nine families a week. They received a lot of complaints from people who did not like all the rules, or from the people who were denied aid. Intake workers heard a lot of strange stories. Turnover was high in Intake, but no higher than in any other section.

The job sounded interesting to me, because there were no quotas, and after thirty days, the Intake worker transfered all eligible cases to the Ongoing units.

I had not wanted Intake when I began work with the Department. I wanted to be involved with my cases over a long period. Not now, however. I would go to Intake. Clients in and out in thirty days.

The phone rang loudly, disturbing my thoughts. I picked up the receiver.

"Yes."

"There's a Lopez down here."

"I have twenty clients named Lopez. Would you ask her her first name?"

"Hold on . . . Lopez!" the clerk screamed into the waiting area.

"Lopez!" she screamed once again.

Finally, she located her.

"Mrs. Lopez, what is your first name?"

"Anita."

"Hello, it's Anita."

"O.K."

I went to the next room, opened the gray file drawer, and pulled out her case record. I flipped to the most recent page, read the write-up, and tried to discover why she was here:

4-16-77

AP-2 completed. TD 06531 is for notice of review and WIN code change.

(1) Cl. had to send away for birth certif. on Hector, Dan, and John. Noted as outstanding & requested within 2 weeks, or delete from budget.

(2) NFL #10 issued to decrease to 326.20, eff 5/4. P.R.P. #1's issued in order to increase protective rent to 125.00, eff 5/1.

(3) Change WIN code on Edward to 11 (ill-90 days). ER 1 updated & SS-32 received.

I could not figure it out. I went down the stairs to the first floor to see her. I had met her once before but had forgotten what she looked like. I was forced into loudly calling her name in the filled waiting room. I never got used to this. I never liked to shout. For example, if I get off a bus and the driver closes the door and is about to leave, and I see a person running to catch the bus, I have to think twice about raising my voice and yelling, "Hold the bus!" Sometimes, I pretend that I do not see the person.

Mrs. Lopez came up to me. She was holding a young child in her arms, and she was about seven months pregnant. According to the case record, she had four other children.

"Hello, do you speak English?"

She shook her head no.

I motioned her to an interviewing room off the main corridor. The room was green and had two metal desks and an old wooden desk, all facing the walls. The wooden desk was free. She sat down in a chair next to the desk. I sat close to her on a squeaky wooden swivel chair. There were seven other people in the stark room, two workers and five clients.

I motioned again to Mrs. Lopez by putting up my index finger and shaking it and my head a little, while mouthing the words "I'll be back in a minute." I had gotten into this ridiculous habit of whispering to Spanish-speaking clients in order to make them understand English.

I walked back down the corridor and asked the clerk at the front desk if he would interpret for me. He said he was too busy. A few more tries to find an interpreter failed, so I went back and tried to speak to Mrs. Lopez.

"Mrs. Lopez, what is it?" I hoped she would understand this phrase.

"Me . . . door."

"Your door?"

"Si, me door."

I looked into the case record for some clue to what she was saying, but found none.

"What about . . . uh, que es . . . uh, what about your door?"

"Me door, si."

"Mrs. Lopez, this is not working." I shook my head and finger at her once again, a little more rapidly this time, and went into the corridor.

I located an eleven year old girl who was there to interpret for her mother.

"Would you help me for a moment?"

She said yes and told her mother she would be right back. The mother looked anxiously at her daughter and indicated that she should hurry back.

With the young girl's help, I learned that Mrs. Lopez's refrigerator door had fallen off the day before. She was here to have it replaced.

Once again I looked into the case record, and discovered that Mrs. Lopez had used her Emergency Assistance nine months earlier to pay an overdue gas bill.

I turned to the girl.

"Tell Mrs. Lopez that she could get the door replaced under Emergency Assistance but that she has already used it once this year. Tell her she can only use it once a year, and she used it for her gas nine months ago."

A long conversation followed between the two of them. The girl looked at me, somewhat agitated.

"She says she needs a door."

"Tell her there is nothing I can do for her for three more months." I held up three fingers.

Upon hearing this Mrs. Lopez began to sob.

I told them both to wait a minute. I went upstairs. First, I checked for phone messages. Two white slips with clients' names and arrows pointing downward were stuck onto the dial . . . two people downstairs to see me.

I quickly filled out a service referral form on Mrs. Lopez and brought it to the Service unit, where I placed it in a wire basket. I went back to the interviewing room and told Mrs. Lopez that I had referred her to services and that she would see a service worker soon. I said that I did not know what they could do for her.

"Please ask Mrs. Lopez to go back to the waiting room."

Mrs. Lopez left the room. I thanked the girl, who returned to her mother. Climbing the stairs to my room, I was sorry that nothing could be done. More than that, I felt angry that Mrs. Lopez had so many children.

IV

The morning continued to be busy. After I saw the two clients downstairs, two calls came in regarding lost checks, which I tried to trace downtown. A woman came in to have her housing application signed. Another wanted a bed for her child, but she was not eligible for one. She was angry, so we talked for a few minutes. A hospital secretary called to inquire about Medicaid eligibility of two children. I checked the case and the computer files. I informed her that they were eligible.

At about 10:30 Rick came down for our break. No one was waiting for me downstairs, so we left immediately.

Recently, during our daily morning walks, we had discovered a local tavern. That is where we were headed today. I started the conversation as we walked.

"I'm thinking of going to Intake."

"Again?"

"I put in a request a few days ago."

"Mike, what do you want Intake for? There's a lot of pressure down there."

"Anything to get out of A.P."

"Yuh, but Mike, what if some real bastard takes your place? At least in A.P. you can help people sometimes."

"We do shit for people. Besides, I'm beginning to think that people should handle their own problems."

"Intake is worse, Mike, I'm tellin' you. I was there for two years."

"Eh, I'll just wait and see what happens. Maybe I won't get it anyway."

We turned down the quiet side street toward the tavern.

We arrived at the tavern. It was not very crowded in the morning. We sat at one of the booths. There was a small window at the far end of the bar where one could order food from the sub shop next door. While Rick got the drinks, I ordered a slice of pizza for myself and an egg salad sub for him.

I brought the food back to the booth. Rick had a beer. I ordered a shot of tequila, with salt and a slice of lemon on the side. I licked the side of my hand, poured the salt on the moistened skin, and then licked it off. I downed half the shot and sucked on the lemon. Rick sipped his beer.

"How's your new supervisor?" Rick asked. I noticed a bit of yellow and white egg salad in his mustache.

"Oh, he's o.k."

"You know, Mike, I feel a lot more comfortable when my supervisor isn't around. She's really all right, but I just feel better, you know, less pressure, when she's out."

"Yeah."

"That Davis is a real bastard. He never compromises. I tell you, Mike, he's just like a stone wall. He hates my guts. You think he has something against you because you helped me on that grievance?"

"I don't know, probably."

I drank the rest of the tequila while Rick finished his beer and had another. I had a blackberry brandy. Usually we only had one drink each, and sometimes we just had subs and cokes. Today we both felt like getting high.

Rick checked his watch, and we had to go. I drank the brandy quickly and it made me cough, but it felt good and warm. Two drinks were enough to set me off.

We stepped outside into the harsh light. Just then I noticed what a pleasant day it was — cool, light breeze, partly cloudy. The only weather I liked better was overcast and drizzly.

We walked back slowly. The area was busy with traffic. Electric street cars and buses ran through frequently. There were a lot of people walking along the main street.

The neighborhood was colorful. There were a number of hospital complexes and universities in the square at one end of the long main street, with the accompanying array of small businesses — inexpensive fast food restaurants, dry cleaners, drug stores. On the side street nearest the office, a dilapidated housing project and a modern, expensive highrise apartment complex stood directly opposite each other. Next to our office stood a huge, old-world stone church, a gymnasium, a small library, an elementary school, and a tiny park with benches and a view of the city skyline. At the other end of the main street, there were mostly vacated apartment buildings and boarded up stores. Only one or two businesses remained open on the block — a small shoe repair store, a discount tire store.

I always enjoyed our walks around the neighborhood because of the different sights. And today the weather was so comfortable and the alcohol had lifted my spirits considerably. I thought back over the morning's events and recounted my experiences with my clients. They all had their problems and I was able to help a few of them. I tried to remember the way they looked, how they spoke, their quirks. Briefly, I felt moved by my work.

We stopped at the park for a few minutes, and I watched the pigeons fly from the roof of the building diagonally across the street to the rectangular patch of grass to my right. An old man, on his daily rounds, had scattered a bag of white bread on the ground for them. I enjoyed watching them eat and then fly back to their home on the dirty building ledge.

Rick got up. "I gotta get back, Mike."

"O.k., José."

Rick and I re-entered the office. My spirit fell. I kept my head down as we walked through the lobby, hoping that no one would call my name. The alcoholic glow was fading, and I felt irritable. Someone touched my arm gently. It was Carol, one of my General Relief clients.

Carol had been attacked by a man in a hallway a few years ago. Her mouth was badly scarred and her teeth were crooked and misshapen. She was tall, very thin, and had beautiful green eyes and frizzy light reddish-brown hair. She spoke very, very softly with a slight drawl, and when she spoke, gave the impression that she was telling you a secret. Her lip and cheek make-up flashed too darkly against her translucent skin. She was very nervous.

"Michael, may I speak with you?"

"Uh, Carol . . . hi. Will you wait a minute? I'll be right down. Uh, I'll see you in the end waiting room."

I went upstairs and washed my face in cold water. I dried myself with a stiff, brown paper towel and went downstairs to the waiting room.

"You look so nice today, Michael," Carol said as I sat down.

"I feel good, Carol."

"You know what I wanted to ask you? That heavy girl, what's her name . . . the one who dresses stylish all the time?"

"Pam, I think."

"Well, Pam, she always gives me these weird looks like I'm freaky or something. Do you think she hates me, Michael?"

"I think she's jealous of you because you're skinny or something."

Carol smiled and a reflex caused her hand to shoot up and cover her jagged teeth. She soon relaxed a little and handed me a paper bag.

"I bought you a present."

I opened the bag and found a cellophaned package of Japanese Nori, an edible seaweed. Carol always brought me presents from the health food store.

"Thank you," I said, looking with slight interest at the Nori.

She told me that her doctors at the institute were doing tests on her mouth. They planned an operation in a few months. First they were going to pull most of her teeth. Then they would reconstruct her twisted jaw. She was unsure of anything beyond that. Carol wanted to make sure that I would not cut off her aid until after her operation. She had heard on the radio that the Department was cutting G.R.s off aid.

I assured her that I had no intention of stopping her welfare payments.

Actually, Carol was ineligible for further welfare payments because she was able to work, according to Department standards. I knew that she was extremely self-conscious about her appearance and would not be able to support herself until her mouth was repaired. She might never be able to support herself. The institute was supposed to pay for the operation since her medical coverage was limited. The decision was an easy one for me. I would take no action against her. I told her that if they transferred my caseload again, I would tell her new worker about the situation. "Don't worry," I kept repeating.

She told me that I was nice and intelligent. She asked me to visit her at home, and I said that I would. She told me to write before I came, because on certain days she went to her aunt's boarding house to clean it.

I walked her to the front door and said goodbye. I added, "I'll write you next week." She smiled, her hand moving a sight slower to cover her mouth this time.

<h1 style="text-align:center">V</h1>

A few more clients had arrived while I was talking to Carol. The first wanted her checks sent to the office instead of to her home. The second requested assistance for an overdue gas bill. She asked me if I would call the gas company to make sure they would not shut off her gas. The third client wanted me to write a letter to her bank. She wanted to cash her five-day-old check which her bank would not cash. A fourth needed her budget adjusted to include her newborn child.

I returned to my desk after a trip to the copy machine. I was cleaning my fingernails with a bent paper clip when the phone rang.

"Hello," I said.

"Hello, is this my worker?"

"What's your name?"

"Moore."

"Yes, I'm your worker."

She went on to explain that she had not received her check for two days. I told her that I would have to wait one more day before I could help her, but that I would call downtown to make sure the check was sent out.

"What am I supposed to do for food until tomorrow?"

I could not believe she did not have any food in the house. No matter. The rules said she had to wait three days.

"I'm sorry, but you'll have to wait until tomorrow. If you don't get it then, come in and I'll give you a food order."

She slammed the phone in my ear.

I continued to pick at my nails. I stopped to get a drink of water from the fountain across from my room. The water tasted rusty, but it was cold.

I heard my phone ringing, and rushed back to my desk. It was near lunchtime. If someone was downstairs, I wanted to get through with them as soon as possible. I was "on duty" today, so I had to be back at 1:00 exactly. I became anxious when I had to listen to a client's problem while my lunch time was ticking away. I picked up the phone. It was Rick. He put on a phony voice.

"Hello, this is Mr. Davis. I understand you are unhappy with your present position."

"Yes, that's correct."

"Yes, I see, well, we have a new position for you. We've decided to make you a recipient."

"Thank you sir."

Rick asked me what I was doing for lunch. I told him I only had an hour. He asked if I had brought my baseball glove. I said I had.

We drove to the large field on the hill overlooking another of the housing projects in the area. There was an unkept baseball diamond and a very expansive outfield with ankle-high grass. The field was always deserted and quiet at this time of day.

Rick positioned himself at home plate and I ran to the outfield. His first few hits were shallow, so I moved in. Soon, he found his swing and the softball was flying over my head.

"Hit 'em higher, Rick."

He was sending me all over the field. He was powerful and enjoyed hitting. I liked running around chasing the ball.

He sent a high drive to my right. I ran for it, the grass swishing at my feet. I crossed my glove arm over my right shoulder and snagged it in the webbing. Rick had his glove on and was crouched at the plate. Play at the plate, I told myself. Cut the runner down. I fired the ball to him. It bounced in front of him to his left and skipped to the backstop.

About ten to one, Rick waved me in. Although it was cool, I was sweating. I put on my shirt over my dampened t-shirt. We did not have time to sit on the bench and relax.

Rick talked about work on the way back. He let me out of his car in front of the building, said "See yuh later," and drove off.

I walked up the stairs and went immediately to the toilet. I washed my face and hands in cold water, ran my fingers through my hair, and returned to my room.

I checked the phone. No messages. No one waiting. I shoved my glove into the bottom drawer of my desk. The other workers in the unit had left for the day. Since I was "on duty", I would have to see their clients. I was hoping for a quiet afternoon in order to complete some paperwork.

After the lunch time work out, I felt sharp. The idea of filling out forms did not bother me. I sometimes lapsed into the mood for a while. I developed a safe, secure attitude. As long as the proper amount of paperwork was done, the administration would leave me alone. Meeting the quota became a personal challenge. People and their situations were not that important in this process. I wanted to make sure that nobody got away with anything. I was saving the state money. Davis called it "joining the winning team."

After a few days, however, two weeks at the most, my attitude would change. I would become short-tempered and restless. I despised the System — the quotas, the forms, my diminishing spirit, independence and patience. I saw as few clients as possible. I was curt and rude to those around me. I tore up useless forms. I ignored anonymous callers who told me that certain clients of mine were cheating the government. I was glad that someone was beating this stifling, lifeless System.

Finally, I would sink into a state of listless, automatic activity, working without feeling or caring. Then the cycle would soon begin over again.

This afternoon, however, I felt sharp. I had had a good amount of exercise, and the morning had been tolerable. I picked up one of the thick cases on my desk and began to fill out some papers.

I was able to work for a long time, uninterrupted. At about 2:30, I called the front desk.

"Hold any clients for about five minutes. I'm going across the street."

"R-r-r-ight," the clerk droned.

I bolted across the street to the sub shop. I picked up a tuna fish sub with lettuce and tomatoes, a bag of potato chips, a ginger ale, and bolted back.

I opened the submarine sandwich at my desk, getting a thick glob of mayonnaise on my palm. Just as I was headed for the sink, the phone rang. I grabbed it with my clean hand.

"Yuh?"

"There's a Mr. Martin down here to see you. He's Linda's client."

"O.k. be right down."

I quickly washed my hand, went into the next room, opened the file cabinet, and rifled through the Martin case. The latest write-up was not too informative.

I went down the stairs to see Mr. Martin. He was standing by the front door, supporting himself with a cane. One look and I knew he was going to give me trouble.

"Mr. Martin, I'm taking Mrs. Snyder's place today. Would you follow me?"

He did not follow. He stood his ground and began speaking:

"I didn't get my food stamps. I can't get around at all and I'm hungry. I've been waiting two weeks for the goddamn things. Where the hell are they?"

I persisted.

"Mr. Martin, would you please follow me to the interviewing room?"

He followed grudgingly.

Once in the room, I asked him to be seated. There were two clients seated at separate desks, waiting for their workers.

I remained standing, one foot on the chair, his case on my thigh, looking through the record. The details were unclear, but I was preoccupied anyway. I was irritated by his manner, and my voice betrayed my irritation when I spoke:

"Mr. Martin, since you're not my case, it's a little hard to tell what's going on here."

I looked down at the case once more and without looking up, continued:

"The delay probably . . ." and he cut me off . . .

"Don't give me that shit! Shut up and get your supervisor now!"

I looked at him dumbly.

"Go ahead! Get him now, shithead!"

I left the room without a word. I walked up the stairs and into the supervisor's office.

"There is a man downstairs. You'll have to see him. I can't handle him."

I handed the supervisor the case and briefly explained the situation.

"I'll see what I can do, Mike," he said, as he left the room.

I walked over to the file cabinets. In a rage, I kicked at an open drawer. Sometimes, when a drawer's rollers were old and rusty, my leg would recoil with a dull thud, and the drawer would hardly move at all. This drawer had been well oiled and it slammed hard.

I returned to my desk and continued with my lunch, my hand shaking slightly as I lifted the can of ginger ale to my mouth.

The supervisor returned a few minutes later and told me that everything was straightened out. All I could stupidly say was:

"That's good, 'cause I felt like killing the jerk."

He began to talk the situation over with me, but the phone interrupted us.

"Talk to you later, Mike."

"Sure, Frank . . . Hello."

"Yes . . . are you a social worker?"

"Yes, I am."

"Oh good. Yes . . . I have a question that I was wondering if you could answer?"

"Go ahead."

"Yes . . . well my friend who's on welfare is getting more food stamps than me and I was wondering why this was?"

"Do you and your friend have the same number of children?"

"Yes, we do."

"Well, all I can say is that the amount of food stamps you receive is based on many different things — like the amount of rent you pay, other household expenses, number of children . . . it seems to me that you and your friend must have different expenses."

"No, we both live in the housing projects and pay the same rent."

"Do you have any other income?"

"No, just the welfare."

"Well, maybe your friend's worker has made a mistake in figuring her budget."

"No, she had it checked, and it's correct."

"What's your last name?"

"Lewis."

"Well, Mrs. Lewis, your worker is out for the afternoon. But I'll put a note on her desk to check your food stamps tomorrow morning and call you."

"I don't have a phone."

"Where are you calling from?"

"My friend's house."

"Can you be reached there tomorrow?"

"No, no one . . . wait a minute . . . no, no one will be here tomorrow."

"How about if your worker sends you a letter explaining your food stamps?"

"That would be all right, I guess."

"Look, Mrs. Lewis, she'll send you the letter and if you're still wondering about it, come in and your worker will sit down with you and go over it. Does that sound o.k.?"

"Yes, that would be all right, then. So . . . I'll wait for the letter and if I'm not satisfied, I should come up to see my worker."

"That's right, either your worker or the worker on duty."

"Alright, then, I'll wait to hear from Miss Peters. And thank you very much, now."

"You're welcome. Goodby."

I hung up the phone, finished the can of ginger ale, and tossed it in the waste basket. I felt drowsy. I gave my green vinyl swivel chair a lazy turn towards the window. Then I crossed my legs on top of the dusty, long silver radiator and stared out the window.

At the right side of the window were a few small trees with pink and white blossoms. Across the narrow main street was a vacant lot where the neighborhood dogs played. There was usually a good show going on there between five or six mongrels. Today the lot was empty. To the left of and in back of the lot, there were old, three-story wooden and brick apartment houses. To the right of the lot was the Clutch Works.

Cars and trucks arrived all day to pick up and deliver transmissions, tailpipes, batteries, and other automotive supplies. A driveway circled around the low, long, yellow brick building. All vehicles were supposed to enter on the right side of the building and exit on the left, but some reversed the process and, due to the frequent arrivals and departures and the necessity of having to exit onto the busy main street, complicated traffic jams often occurred. Today, however, the Clutch Works was as quiet as the vacant lot.

I clasped my hands behind my neck, stared out into space, and thought about nothing in particular. After a short time, I unclasped my hands, rubbed my left eye with the heel of my left hand, threw my head back, and yawned widely.

I turned the chair back to face my desk, opened one of the case records, and began to fill out a computer release. After it was completed, I ripped out the two sheets of carbon paper and threw them into the basket. I placed one of the carbon copies into the case record, one in the clerk's file in the room across the hall and the original on top of the case, fastened with a paper clip. I brought the case into the supervisor's office and left it on his desk to be checked.

I returned to my desk, opened another case, and began the same procedure. When the office was quiet and there were no interruptions, the process was very tranquilizing. I took great care with my printing and displayed a neat style. I ripped off the carbon sheets carefully at the perforations. I folded the papers crisply.

The case before me was 3 folders thick, which usually meant that the client had a long and active history with the Department. I flipped back through the pages out of curiosity. I stopped at a page dated 12-28-47 and read the write-up:

12-28-47

Phyllis is a medium-sized, neat appearing woman of somewhat limited intelligence. She remained in the city until she was 9 yrs. old, attending school thru the 4th grade. Her parents then took her back home to live with a relative. After attending school for a month or two, she left to assist with household & farm duties. She returned to the city at the age of 19. Here she entered employ. as a domestic. As places of employment were changed frequently, she failed to recall correct names & addresses of employers. Her last employment was day work, for approximately a yr. She became a recipient of General Relief in June of last year. She applied for A.F.D.C. two years ago but was rejected because of failure to provide necessary documenting requirements. She asserts that she managed to get her few articles of furniture from junk dealers and friends. She insists that her husband returned home for only one night, last year. She permitted him to stay overnight without question as she thought that he had come to remain. He left the next morning and has not been seen or heard from since. As a result of the visit, a baby was reported to have been conceived.

Mrs. Collins, Social Worker

I flipped the pages ahead and stopped at 3-13-65:

3-13-65

Worker calls at client's address. The apt. is neat and clean. The rental is paid to date with exception of $5.00. According to client she has not been feeling well lately. The client complains of Migraine headaches and states she has been tired most of the time. According to the client, the children enjoy good health, but Stephen needs an eye examination and dental care. Joan, who suffers from a nervous condition which makes her fidgety, is going to the hospital upon the advice of the school nurse. Jackie has a hearing problem and is seen at a local hospital. He is being taught lip reading at a local school. Some people state the boy should have a hearing aid but the doctors feel that he should be taught lip reading. Jackie recently won an award (certificate of merit) from an art contest, and his school has put him up for candidacy at a local art school. The boy does well in math, but poorly in English probably due to his hearing difficulty. The client herself and the rest of the children have an excellent command of the English language. The client wrote a poem for Stephen which was submitted to his school, this was not strictly honest but the boy won a small amount of money. The client showed the worker some of her poems which in the worker's opinion displayed a marked flare for writing. The worker tries to encourage client to submit poems to her local newspapers.

Mrs. Kramer, Social Worker

I was flipping to a more recent date when the phone rang. It was the head administrative clerk.

"Michael, Mr. Davis would like to see you in his office."

"O.k. I'll be right there. Thanks."

I closed the case and went immediately to his room. The door was opened. Davis was seated at his desk, head down, signing papers. He was an impressive-looking man — squarely built, strong features, tough, dissheveled appearance. He had an aggressive manner.

I stood at the doorway, wondering how to get his attention. He looked up and motioned me in.

I sat facing him. I looked up at an ivy plant hanging from a green pipe running across the ceiling. He finished signing a paper, put down his pen, pushed his swivel chair away from his desk at a slight angle, and leaned back.

"Mike, I have received your memo requesting a transfer to Intake. Why do you want to leave an easy job like A.P.?"

"I need a change, a new experience within the Department, and Intake sounds challenging."

Davis went on:

"People work hard at Intake. There are strict deadlines to meet down there. It's a lot different from A.P., because you have to get the work done within a certain time period."

"I know. I've talked to a few people about it."

"Mike, I've got to post the job for two weeks to see if anyone else is interested. Besides, I can't let you go until I'm sure they'll fill your slot."

"I talked to Joe Cummings downstairs, and he said he'd be willing to switch with me."

"Well, I don't know about that. I'll have the position posted. Get back to me in a few weeks."

I thanked him for his time and left, feeling certain that he would not give me the transfer.

I sat in my room and stared out the window for a long time. Felix the janitor came in and shut off the lights.

"Time to go home, kid."

I got up, checked the neat piles of cases on my desk for tomorrow's work, walked down the stairs and out the front door.

Halfway home, stopped in traffic, my Plymouth stinking of exhaust fumes, I remembered that I had left my baseball glove in the unlocked bottom drawer of my desk. I wondered if I'd see it again.

CHAPTER THREE

SOCIAL SERVICES

We are the hollow men
We are the stuffed men
Leaning together
Headpiece filled with straw. Alas!
Our dried voices, when
We whisper together
Are quiet and meaningless
As wind in dry grass
Or rats' feet over broken glass
In our dry cellar

—T.S. Eliot
"The Hollow Men"

I. Front Line Services Workers — Orientation and Climate: An Underview

Most people probably have a fair understanding as to the significance of this book's title: *Public Welfare: Notes From Underground.* But certainly a number of people may be unaware as to just how underground the welfare social worker actually is. To show *all* of the actual connections of governmental and extra-governmental influence and authority over the social worker would require a great amount of space as well as a great amount of insight. Each of the offices of government and each division within the Department ultimately involved in the provision of "social welfare" to the public is an entity unto itself. Each has significant, if varying degrees of, power. Each has something important to say about the shaping of Welfare policy, procedures, service delivery models, staff size, job duties, etc. Some affect the activities of front line welfare workers by means of enacting laws, writing policy and procedural rules, and by passing a state budget.[1] The control and allocation of funds for Welfare is by far the most direct and tangible means of determining the Department's operation. This appears to be especially true now since the passage of Proposition 13 in California and the wave of public sentiment since then calling for closer restrictions on state spending.

Complex interdependency is commonplace for Massachusetts state government and for an administrative agency like the Department of Public Welfare. As everyone knows, this interdependency is the stuff of which "red-tape" is made. Social workers within the system do not expect this to change substantially; nor do they expect their position in the 'great chain' to shift or be altered in any great way. Ironically, however, the incredibly complex and intricate structure exists for a relatively simple purpose; that purpose is to enable the front line direct service social worker to provide concrete services to people in need.

It is this enabling ability which should be the *true* measure of an administrative agency. After all, almost no one above the lowest level provides a single direct welfare service to an eligible client. If the family social worker is unable to do his job, the administration exists in a vacuum.

We have said that no *substantial* change is expected when, at the same time, Massachusetts is about to embark on a plan to develop a brand new public social services agency. Despite the efforts of some Massachusetts legislators and Department officials who have succeeded in mandating the creation of this new and comprehensive public social service agency, the Department of Social Services,[2] most family workers have consistently acknowledged that the only *genuine* remedy to problems in the state's present Office of Social Services will require a substantial increase in the number of State social workers and a substantial increase in their salaries.[3] Social workers almost never look to ingenious management models for improvement in the work they do. Adequate salaries and incentives to stay and persever with difficult work appear to them to be the obvious starting-places for instituting change. Obviously, since it is at their level that the work takes place it is only rational, in the minds of social service workers, that salutary change occur there. This would mean a huge expenditure of state funds. But without these basic remedies, changing the name and organizational structure of the Office of Social Services can only promise to briefly disguise the front-line service deficiencies which workers experience daily. Veteran family workers in Massachusetts (and there are too few of them remaining) have experienced the metamorphoses from Division of Child Guardianship to Division of Family and Children's Services to the Office of Social Services. Many feel it has been change for its own sake without any significant improvement in the workers' ability to effect change within disturbed families.

It must be granted that everyone loves to criticize the Department of Public Welfare and the Office of Social Services. For many insiders and outsiders, it is a national pasttime. Social Services has been studied to death; criticisms have been leveled against it a hundred-fold. Of course the disturbing thing is that many of the criticisms are legitimate:

> The Department of Public Welfare has been in a continuous state of transition since the state takeover eight years ago. They have two major responsibilities: assistance payments to eligible clients and social services to families and children. This dual role produces an irreconcilable management conflict model — the clear loser is social services to children and families. The priority of DPW is cash payments. Social services, for all practical purposes, are drifting out of control. The various social service programs consist of $63.8 million dollars of purchased services — the cost of administering those programs exceeds $13 million dollars. During the past two years, there have been three Assistant Commissioners for Social Services, a fact that seriously hampered central policy and direction. The turnover and turn-around of central staff has likewise contributed to a lack of direction for the agency.
>
> The level of morale among the social services staff throughout the state would be disturbing to even the most casual observer.
>
> Programs for children who need day care, foster care, group care, and protective services are often successful only because individual social workers and administrators endure. They manipulate the agency disorganization to get some children services. For their efforts, they receive little support.[4]

This quotation is taken from the February, 1977 report, *The Children's Puzzle*, a study of children's services commissioned by the State Legislature. Most workers, I believe, regard the report as a fair representation of the various state-run children's services agencies. The Children's Services Task Force goes on to recommend:

> The Department of Public Welfare should be abolished. All social service programs should be transferred to a new department to be

named the Department of Human Development. All assistance payments programs should be transfered to a new department to be named the Department of Economic Security. The new department should include 2 divisions: The Division of Employment Security and the Division of Family and Individual Assistance.[5]

Apart from the controversies which the *Children's Puzzle* stimulated at every level, it is important to point out that the report was organized around the principle of financial austerity: the report's position is that the state can do more with its present state services without engendering fiscal irresponsibility. What has social workers worried and cynical about improvements *on paper* is that front-line working conditions and the need for adequate salaries will continue forever to be neglected. When austerity and accountability are stressed, social workers know that they and their clients will be among the hardest hit. They are confident that if the Proposition 13 advocates take up the ax against public spending, Public Welfare social workers will be set back to a financially unrecoverable distance in their effort to win reasonable working conditions and equitable salaries.

It is important to understand that our public social workers make up a very unstable labor force. Obviously it is very difficult to achieve stability when over 50% of the members of a group are different from year to year. Also, in times of restricted public spending, Public Welfare social services, lacking a strong and organized support group, can be expected to be among the first victims of budgetary cut-backs. Despite the desires of well-meaning welfare observers to see the Welfare Department's range of services eliminated or more restricted than they presently are, one fact remains: large *administrative agencies* like the Department of Public Welfare simply cannot be made to go so far as to close up shop. Although the worker turnover rate is great, the Department itself is not a temporary or, for that matter, an especially unstable governmental edifice. Because the Department is founded on fundamentally essential and far-reaching public services, the Department itself will survive almost any external and internal administrative catastrophe. Catastrophies on the social worker level such as high turnover rate, morale paralysis or the like, which might eliminate effective delivery of tangible services, do not have the effect of seriously threatening the existence of the Department as an institution.

Whatever the *actual* outcome of the recent advocacy and deliberations within the Legislature on these questions, it is vital that

the importance and value of the Department of Public Welfare
and its employees be recognized. No other state agency has
claimed quite the same territory of human needs: the need for
money and family-life services. Private, *ad hoc* charity will never
work. Happily, the Department of Public Welfare is not a charita-
ble organization. Rather, it is an effort to make democratic the
distribution of money and services to those of us who need and
have guaranteed rights to these things. This we need to have in
mind even in our sharpest criticisms.

The job of the Department social worker is, I believe, without
rival in terms of its stresses, dangers, level of difficulty, and
significance. In this chapter I shall analyze several issues arising
from personal experience; they are, I am sure, issues which
transcend their being important only to one person. The specific
experiences which are described may be regarded as generally
expressive of the encounters of any service workers. None of us
can lay claim to exclusiveness of such experiences or of the issues
they raise. Nearly every worker who has done family work will
recognize here his own experiences, some quite disturbing. However, I do not propose to transmit a catalogue of common misery.
Rather I propose better to elucidate the job, clearing away as
much of the cant and jargon of the profession as possible, and by
presenting a clear and felt understanding of the examples and
issues at hand.

The social worker responsible for social service cases is overworked, underpaid, undervalued, and overwhelmed. The work
location and physical working conditions are generally the same
as for the Assistance Payments social worker, already described.
Physical conditions in most locations are crowded, make-shift,
dirty and depressing. City offices are worse than rural offices; city
cases are worse than rural cases; city families have more to trouble
them, while rural families have troubles without the resources to
help them. Often, the hardships even out. Worker and family
face handicaps together; the worker's high caseload is as much a
handicap to the family as it is to the worker; a paucity of (or
incompetency of) community resources is a bane to both family
and worker. In the long-run, every worker comes to know that he
can truly be useful to only a handful of families over periods of
years. The likelihood of workers coming to this perception contributed, I am sure, to the fact that ninety-one percent of the
Boston region's social service staff left their jobs during fiscal year
1976.

At the time of this writing, I have worked as a social worker in Boston for five years. I have been relocated to different offices three times. During the time I performed direct family work, seventeen child welfare service co-workers came and went in my units. I have worked in these five years under the direction of five different supervisors; I am presently working under the direction of my third Commissioner of Public Welfare. Concurrent with many of these changes, my direct family caseload had been either dramatically "shuffled" or wholly changed four times.

Mine is not a unique case; service workers, like their counterparts in Assistance Payments, quickly learn that their caseloads and their job assignments are subject to administrative interference and manipulation from all sides.

II. Screening and Assigning Cases: ·
   Service Worker Vulnerability

From July 2, 1973 until September 5, 1974 I was assigned exclusively to child welfare cases in a newly formed service unit which was physically housed at 39 Boylston Street in Boston but responsible for families in the Roxbury/North Dorchester section of the city — a few miles away. Naturally enough, under these circumstances, it was difficult to feel a part of the community our unit served. Feeling a part was made difficult also by the fact that my co-workers and I came from socio-economic backgrounds radically different from those of "our" families. At first blush it all seemed a case of the 'square peg in a round hole' practice of worker-to-job match up.

Because our unit was newly formed, we started at the beginning in all aspects of the job — three or four weeks of social work training given by training specialists from within the Department, followed by visits to neighborhood services programs, mental health facilities, visits to the District, Boston Juvenile, and Probate courts, and several group meetings with our supervisor.

We concentrated on child welfare intake cases — receiving the slim manila folder which contained the basic information from which to begin: name of family, children, presenting problem, name of referring party. During this period, child welfare referrals made to the Boston Region of the Department by outside reporters were first "screened" by Mr. James Sheehan who shared office space with our unit. Jim made the initial determination that (1) the Department was the appropriate resource for the family and (2) that the presenting problem warranted immediate action by a child welfare unit. Inappropriate referrals were routed to private social work agencies. Jim was a man of unparalleled grace and diplomacy. For persons on the outside, Jim made the reporting of child abuse and neglect to the Department a human, reassuring and therapeutic experience. He personified all that was attractive about the Department to a small band of neophyte social workers new to the inside workings of Welfare. My co-workers and I regarded him as a surrogate father and teacher. He was a highly skilled child welfare screening specialist. To the regret of many service workers, Jim's role was phased out over a period of two years from September, 1974 when the Department adopted the "Separated System" under which individual Community Service Area (CSA) offices developed Intake-Referral-Follow Up (IRF) units.

IRF and on-going social service staff then began assuming primary responsibility for screening and determining initial eligibility for child welfare services. Protective service or child welfare intake thereby became subsumed into the much larger aggregate of social services intake determinations. Child welfare lost the concentrated and skilled focus it had once had under Jim, but it also broadened the CSA community base for receiving local abuse and neglect referrals.[6] Appendix XII constitutes the Department's present format for information gathering on abuse/neglect referrals.

With the advent of the "Separated System" my unit moved to the Roxbury Crossing Welfare office. For the next two years attention was focused on coordinating the functions of the newly established IRF units and the newly metamorphosed on-going service units. The on-going service units were named "integrated" units by virtue of the mixed caseloads they handled. An integrated generalist social worker under Separation carried single service, multi-service and child welfare cases. They were informally characterized as "soft" or "hard" services according to the amount of time and level of difficulty each case represented.

A scheme of point values was hammered out which determined case-load size. The only guidance which the State Legislature had given for determining a social worker's caseload could be found in the Massachusetts General Laws, Chapter 18, which cited 180 units as the limit for a social worker's caseload. By itself, 180 units is a meaningless and arbitrary measure. It was left to the Department and the Social Worker's Union to measure its work in finer detail. The following was our unit's scheme:

1 unit	single service case
3 units	multi-service intact family case
4.5 units	foster care service
7 units	child welfare intake
9 units	protective service intake
12 units	51A intake (where a 51A Report of Neglect or Abuse was on file with Central Registry)

There was as much variation in the use of this scheme as there was adherence to it. Everyone recognized that it was an artificial and arbitrary scheme. Neighboring welfare offices developed slightly different point values but experienced the same difficulties in applying values to particular cases. Assigning values was difficult because a wide range of complicating factors continually came into play. To give but one example — what could be the worker's point-count for a family in which a private agency had petitioned the court, custody had been awarded to the Department, the child placed in foster care and an intake study had not yet begun? Would you expect to receive 4.5 units because the child was in foster placement? Or 7 units because you have yet to conduct an intake study? Or 9 units because you believe the child's placement constituted a protective service to the child? As a consequence of problems like this, there was much agonizing over point values — with social workers arguing for a combination of points for complicated cases and the CSA administration advocating the lowest point-count possible per case. The administrators frequently won these skirmishes.

In attempting to reconcile the Separated System with some of the realities of the job, the Roxbury Crossing CSA did something simple and innovative. No sooner was Separation upon us when it became clear that some service workers were ill-equipped to manage child welfare cases. This was either because they had no prior experience in this area or because their mental health was threatening to collapse under the stresses of protective service work. Also, age and physical limitations might have prevented them from safely advancing into dangerous housing projects. The innovation was this: Our CSA created a separate unit made up entirely of single service caseloads, typically "soft" purchased services such as homemaking, chore, daycare and babysitting for eligible intact families and individuals. The model worked well and resulted in the retention of workers who otherwise were headed for burn-out. This innovation probably aided in reducing the number of child welfare cases which were to be later mishandled by untrained staff who joined Social Services units at the time of Separation.

I was assigned to some relatively unusual cases; my colleagues of course faced similar situations. In 1975, a supervisor from my office was under investigation by Department and other state officials for allegedly establishing a fictitious foster parent account and for possible malfeasance in his casework with gay foster children. Published reports disclosed that this supervisor later committed suicide. I was chosen to assume responsibility for two of his cases in which state officials suspected various abuses of social work ethics and violations of law. This supervisor had been an open proponent of special services to gay adolescents; he had approved foster placements in which gay foster children were living with gay foster parents.

For several months I gave these cases special attention — meeting regularly with the children and foster parents involved. Anxiety was running very high in my Department and in the Massachusetts Attorney General's office. The Department, at this time, had provided only vague, tentative policy statements on services to gay children by gay adults. There was talk of possible connections between these cases and others in which gay boys were found to be sexually exploited by abusive gay men. Some of those cases had resulted in the deaths of adolescent children. Much of the Department's apprehension was quite justified and responsible.[7] But some of the apprehension bordered on hysteria and homophobia; some of it was vindictive in tone, aimed at all gay adults caring for children. In this atmosphere I needed to conduct my casework; this now included many surreptitious meetings with detectives from the Attorney General's Office.

After considerable work it was evident to me that my cases had nothing to do with the controversies which surrounded them. In one case, neither the foster parent nor the child was gay. There was very little of the bond between them which one would expect in any caring adult-child relationship, and the child subsequently moved out on his own to work and attend school. They had little idea that they had been the focus of such attention.

In the other case, I found that the foster parent was clearly a very open, caring and responsible gay man. He was an outspoken advocate for gay rights and the foster placement needs of gay adolescents. The foster parent's relationship with the child was in every respect a strong and appropriate relationship. The foster child was himself bi-sexual. He had felt rejected by his step-father and was fearful of the consequences of being placed with a 'straight' family. The three of us discussed these issues individually and with the child's mother who endorsed the plan to continue her son's present placement. All parties in this case were acutely aware of the Attorney General's investigative work and accepted the close scrutiny which they were powerless to avoid.

The cases themselves, then, were relatively trouble-free and innocuous. The circumstances surrounding them, however, were otherwise. Those circumstances pointed out to me not only the vulnerability of gay adolescents who have been turned out of their homes, of gay adults who wished to provide responsible foster care; they clearly revealed the extent of the social worker's own vulnerability — vulnerability to criminal prosecution, administrative intervention by the Department and potentially life-threatening situations from organized crime. Detectives from the Attorney General's Office suspected, and were later shown to be correct in suspecting, organized criminal activities in other cases under their investigation. In my cases, dangerous outcomes were averted, except that I was keenly aware of the ever-present possibilities they could have posed.

Another case, quite different from these, required me to look closely at the question of the legal protection available to social workers. It involved a multi-service case with two major components: (1) the first child born had been in the permanent custody of the Department from the time of his birth and was, at the time of my involvement, twelve years old and soon to be adopted by his foster parents; (2) his siblings — sisters, aged five and seven — were living with their mother and in need of therapeutic day care services. I had been working with the children's mother in order to help her resolve some of her conflicts around 'losing' her first child to the Department. I was also aiming to strengthen the relationship she had with her daughters. Arrangements were made by the mother for her daughters to be placed under the care of an adult male family day-care provider/baby sitter while the mother was at work.

I made several telephone calls to the sitter and received no answer. I made unscheduled visits to his home and observed that his apartment was poorly furnished and that there was very little in the way of toys or games to entertain children. On two visits there had been no response to my knocking on the door though I could hear activity inside. In the course of a week I learned from the children and their mother that the sitter was sexually abusing the girls and had threatened to hurt them if they told their mother. Alarmed by this, I stopped all payments to the sitter, made other day-care arrangements for the children, and made further inquiries. I learned from local police, from neighbors, and from the Office for Children that reports of this type had been known to them in other cases where girls had been placed in this sitter's care, but that no parents or agency personnel were willing to follow through and testify in a court complaint because these people feared a counter-suit of slander or libel. The children's testimony, alone, would not be enough. Further, the sitter had the legal resources available to delay, and effectively block, the revocation of his day-care license which he had obtained from the Office for Children; and so, the Office for Children was in a bind. From my point of view, it would be unconscionable for me not to act and not to pursue the revocation of the sitter's license; but, to act would mean testifying against him in court on the basis of hearsay evidence, and that from young children.

Facing the possibility of a counter-suit for libel, I sought the advice of attorneys from within the Department and was advised that in this case, and *many* others, the Department would not provide workers with an agency or private attorney. Legal service would be at my own expense. The only conceivable alternative would be for the Department to refer the matter to the Attorney General's Office, but the Attorney General's Office was under no obligation to provide such a service. It was common knowledge that the Attorney General's Office would assume responsibility for defending the Department's social workers only in those cases which promised to be interesting or controversial tests of law. I was therefore out on a limb.

As it happened, the sitter did threaten to counter-sue; but he left the city shortly before his own scheduled trial. The court case against him was dropped, the children had been placed in a day-care center and I was relieved of the need to anticipate and provide my own defense. The point had been driven home, however; social workers for the Department must expect and often encounter great financial and personal risks in the normal course of their work.

On June 9, 1978, Welfare Commissioner Alexander E. Sharp II sent a memo to Department staff advising them of Senate bill 1528:

In its present form, the legislation would immunize state employees acting within the scope of their employment from any liability for their actions or failure to act provided that those actions or ommissions were not the result of *gross* negligence, malice, corruption, fraud or bad faith. Further, once it is known that the Commonwealth has assumed liability for its employees, frivolous lawsuits against individual workers will be discouraged.

The bill passed in July, 1978 and applies to lawsuits arising from incidents which occurred on or after August 16, 1977. On July 20, 1978, Commissioner Sharp advised Department staff:

In addition to immunizing employees against liability for all negligent acts or ommissions performed within the scope of their employment, this bill now authorizes the Commonwealth to pay for the legal fees and the damages (up to one million dollars) awarded in claims where the employee and not the Commonwealth is liable.

III. The Case Record: Containing Chaos

There are several ways of looking at a social service family case record. To get the feeling of working at the job, the reader should place himself in the Welfare office in imagination: He ignores the cacophony of ringing phones, clacking typewriters, extraneous conversations and AM radio signal noise which greet him. He sits at his desk, gets comfortable. Now he takes a case record from atop the desk and places it on his lap. There it is: a plain, worn manilla folder — a tab on the top — last name of the family and a child welfare case number scribbled on the tab. So far so good. Next, he grasps the record with both hands, raises it from his lap and estimates its weight — a pound and a half? two pounds? More? Well, how can this be?

He has just arrived, he hasn't done anything with this family yet; there are two pounds of information facing him already. After all, he can't imagine gathering two pounds of information on his *own* family and suddenly he realizes that his personal sense of "proportions" didn't prepare him for this. Next, he places the record on the desk and opens it. There they are: two or three hundred individual sheets of paper — mostly white sheets, some blue. Some pages are numbered, many are not. There are a few 5 x 7 inch cards, a dozen or more folded sheets of paper, staples and paper clips galore. Some of the papers are virtually illegible — some smudged, some are nearly blank xeroxed copies of missing originals. He starts thinking: this is not a case record, it's a twelve pound turkey dressed with twenty pounds of stuffing.

The case record before him probably represents ten to twenty years of work with this family performed by ten to twenty social workers. He has inherited decades of interviews, home visits, court appearances, correspondence of innumerable kinds, address changes, foster home placements, births, deaths, fires, rapes, abandonments, abuse, neglect and provider authorizations. On first glimpse he cannot make any more sense out of this record than out of a psychotic episode.

It is fair to say that until recently case record management has not been a mainstay of the Department's Office of Social Services. Many social workers have felt and still feel that the record itself should be of only minor concern. Usually this is companion to the view that social workers are able to keep the essential information and casework issues straight in their heads or in their personal notes; and, since workers do not generally bring the case record with them on home visits or to court, in fear of losing it or risking loss of confidentiality, they need not be concerned with the cosmetic value of a presentable, organized record. In short, the folder has historically been a receptacle for whatever has *seemed* to belong in it. In many ways, it is easy to understand this point of view. Just imagine the social worker taking upon himself the task of organizing fifty or more family case records. In February, 1977, when I left family case work, I was terminating my relationship with fifty-six families or individuals. Even though I had been working to organize my records for several months, I was far from completing the work. Nevertheless, a little neurotic compulsion, I had decided, was preferable to fifty-six possible psychotic breaks.

In February of 1978, the Office of Social Services published a comprehensive system for family case review. The review system had been principally designed by a Central Office administrator who had a thorough background in child welfare; he had been a social service supervisor in the Boston region before undertaking administrative responsibility for the Case Review System. His format for case record organization is included as Appendix XIII. It is the first serious attempt by the Office of Social Services to organize its huge volume of case records. It is included here to give readers an idea of the materials and work involved in setting up and maintaining a family case record.

A specific child welfare agency record will not necessarily resemble one of another agency; but the record, whatever its organization, should be a casework tool. The organization of individual case records not only assists case workers in mastering feelings of helplessness: it helps to more effectively serve the clients. The case worker can go to the record with some measure of confidence that he will be able to locate information quickly: he can be assured that the information will not only be there but that it will be reliable as well. It is a clear instance of one social work function favorably affecting another: the administrative role affecting the casework role.

The Group Care Unit undertook the organization of its 1800 case records in August of 1977. A Child Record Entry Worksheet (CREW) was printed up in one hundred sheet pads and distributed to unit members. A CREW sheet (Appendix XIV) was attached to the inside of the record cover to facilitate case record dictation. Whenever the record was removed from the file drawer, the worker wrote his case action onto the CREW: after many uses, or when the sheet was full, the worker could then submit the record to a secretary for typing. It was a very simple mechanism and it assisted in competent case management. It was especially valuable in circumventing the need to submit the entire record for typing services every time the worker had dictation to enter. It began to solve an age-old problem common to the Department and other large agencies — the tendency to develop complicated and intricate procedures when a simple one would suffice.

If the contents of a case record serve to reflect the dynamics of a family, it is also true that the condition of the record is an index to the agency's dynamics. If my record is out of control, then I am out of control. Even if no one around me detects the confusions of purpose which I feel from trying to work from an unmanageable record, I know those confusions every time I address my clients, my colleagues, or the courts. No one should encourage such anxiety attacks; in any case, they can and very probably will arise from elsewhere in the job.

IV. Communications Equipment: The Four Senses

1. *The Telephone*

Social workers rely upon four means of gathering and disseminating information: telephones, letters/memoranda, on-site visits, and meetings. Of these mechanisms, the telephone is the most frequently used and at the same time it is the chain's weakest link. I invite you to listen in:

Ring, ring, ring, ring . . . ring, ring — Blip.
"WELFAYUH"

"Hello, Mr. Smith, please, Social Services?"
"Line's busy — you want to ho. . ." — Blip.

It can be an ugly experience. Every frequent caller to a welfare office must become accustomed to a brusque reception followed by the nether world of "hold" — that invisible time and space continuum in which all things coast off into insignificance. It matters not if your call is urgent or casual; whatever your place in the great chain of being, you can be put on "hold." Rest assured, the Commissioner can be put on hold.

The issue really is that the telephone service in most welfare offices is poor; circuits are overloaded, switchboards are old and under-monitored; telephone sets are old and in poor repair. Why should this matter? Why should social workers have nice new telephones? After all, lots of people get by with standard telephone sets. The problem is this: the telephone is a social worker's workhorse. Without dependable telephone service, social workers are reduced in their capacity to work.

Because the use of the telephone is so vital, the instrument *must* be dependable. Forty percent or more of the work day can be taken up with the phone. Much of this time is made useless by virtue of antiquated phone systems. The resultant inefficiency affects nearly every aspect of a social worker's functioning; it has particular impact on his/her reputation in the minds of colleagues and clients as being either dependable or undependable, competent or incompetent. If one is unfortunate enough to work in an office with an especially poor phone system, he may be informally "black-listed" by would-be callers; this means that some calls may not be reaching the worker because people are choosing not to suffer the difficulties of making the call. In short, one's telephone has the power to create a worker's reputation wholly apart from the messages it carries.

My unit at the Roxbury Crossing welfare office had the use of one direct telephone line in addition to four extensions from the office switchboard. The direct line contributed significantly to the receipt of emergency telephone calls. At one time there had been three direct lines to our unit, before two were removed to effect administrative cost savings. In short, the one remaining line enabled us to respond to crises. It added to our unit's response capability but at the same time it often resulted in an overabundance of work to do. This was a mixed blessing, we felt; we were not convinced that the cut-backs had been sensible. Direct telephone lines were *never* added to the switchboard lines connecting other service units in our building.

II. *Letters and Memoranda:*
The Policy and Procedures Manuals

To whom does a social service worker write letters and memoranda? It is easier to inquire after that portion of the population which does *not* receive a letter from a social worker! The volume of letters is staggering, it is in any large public agency. Yet, even more letters would be written if there was an adequate number of secretaries to handle the volume. Many workers type their own letters or simply cut back because they notice that a secretary (who may handle typing for twenty or more social workers) already has four unwieldy, tottering stacks of case records and dictation to handle before reaching their letters. Why bother piling it higher and deeper? Consequently, some important communication does not come to pass.

The generation of administrative letters and memoranda, though, does not encounter the same obstacles. If the Department of Public Welfare is expert at one thing, it is in the proliferation of administrative communications. Policy and Procedures manuals are not static things; they are constantly added to and subtracted from. And this occurs by means of state-wide administrative letters.

The social service worker who is "manually equipped" is in possession of at least four large three-ring binders marked "Assistance Payments Policy Manual," "Office of Social Services Policy Manual," "Office of Social Services Procedures Manual" and a "Child Welfare Policy Manual." One could spend a lifetime organizing, reading, clarifying, amending, opening and closing them. It is almost impossible to pore over and comprehend the manuals alone, never mind apply all of the policies and procedures with consistency or fidelity. It is an extraordinary task for social workers to keep "up to the minute" in all of these areas. Social workers can never be precisely contemporary with the Department's administration.

There can be no certain remedy for this. Workers learn to adapt to it as a way of life and simply receive their bundles of administrative letters, review them for what significance they may hold for the worker's immediate or forseeable concerns and then either keep or discard them. In short, workers exercise their right and need to be selective. No one, it appears, can turn off the waterfall.

III. *On-site visiting: the home visit*

Home visits, or visits to any location for the purpose of seeing a client, are central to the conduct of good casework. In this context, unlike the assistance payments worker, the service worker is less concerned with the matter of strictly determining a client's financial eligibility for a particular service than with assessing a client's social condition and needs. To be sure, there are strict guidelines for service workers to observe in determining some clients' financial eligibility for social services as in the case of a healthy, intact, single parent family in which the parent is employed, is receiving AFDC and is also in need of day-care services while at work.

But, for the most part, service workers look more closely at social rather than financial conditions when seeing a client. There is no greater opportunity for this determination than at the place the client resides or frequently visits. There, the worker has the chance for both an objective and subjective perception of the client. If it is a family of eight living in a four-room apartment in a housing project, you might note that (1) the living space is inadequate; (2) the four range-top gas burners are all turned on because the building heat is off; (3) there is rat poison on the floor and easily accessible to the children in the family; (4) there are paint chips along the edges of the floors below chipped and mottled walls; (5) there are dark, heavy cheesecloth drapes covering broken windows; (6) it is dark inside because there are no floor or wall lamps; (7) it is 11:00 A.M. on a weekday and yet all six school-age children are in the home; (8) there is a man asleep on a couch, which is the only furniture in the living-room; and (9) the woman who answered the door, Mrs. Jones, the mother of the children, and 'girl-friend' of the man on the couch, is saying to you that she has "had it up to here" with nosy social workers who are "trying to take her kids away." These things you cannot get during a hasty meeting with the same client who visits your office.

IV. *Meetings*

If not meeting with a client, the worker is invariably meeting with his supervisor or other workers. Supervision — a one-on-one session between worker and supervisor — usually occurs once a week; at this time the worker's case-count is 'estimated,' new cases assigned, closed cases recorded, court reports reviewed and special problems discussed. Supervision is either formal — agenda items written down, submitted and discussed in order of priority — or informal, where case-related issues are discussed at random. Often, meetings of either type provide the worker with an opportunity to blow off steam, to freely express feelings of frustration with the job. Many supervisors believe, I think rightly, that providing workers with a special time to 'ventilate their feelings' is one of the most valuable services they can offer workers.

Unit meetings consist of open-forum discussions among all of the workers of a particular service unit and their supervisor. They occur usually at two-week intervals; they provide the opportunity to update information about community resources, to discuss the performance and achievement levels of the unit as a whole, to plan visits to existing or new community agencies, and to introduce the most recent administrative changes from within the Department. Not surprisingly, unit meetings, too, are an opportunity to express feelings.

Of course, these things only happen when a service unit consists of two or more members. For a period of two months at the Roxbury Crossing Office I enjoyed the singular honor of being the only person in my unit — no supervisor, no co-workers. The attrition rate of workers for the entire building at the time was estimated to be well above fifty percent, with the majority of these social workers leaving employment from service units. Uncovered service cases in my unit alone amounted to about two hundred and fifty in number; the number was continually growing. Soon, a supervisor was installed and later, one co-worker. But, for a while, I was the Lone Ranger of on-going integrated social services for the whole of Allston/Brighton and Annunciation Road in Roxbury. Together, these areas made up approximately one-fifth of the entire residential area of the city of Boston.

V. The Subjective Correlative

I. *Professionalism vs. personal bias*

Social workers come equipped with feelings. Feeling emotions is the natural and healthy consequence of working at a job in which employees directly encounter the deaths of clients, the physical and emotional neglect, abuse, and abandonment of children. As a result, social workers, if they are to survive in the job, develop a fairly refined knowledge of their nervous systems. One's nervous system is a tool one must work with. A service worker who is "out of touch" with what he is feeling will "burn out" of his job and leave it. Worse, he might soon be headed for serious emotional conflicts.

I recall a co-worker who so thoroughly denied his feelings that he believed God had ordained his employment with the Department as a test of his "right" belief that battered children deserved to be beaten; it had been decided by God, of course, that the battered child be born to battering parents. This worker merely wished to be pointed like an automaton in the direction of troubled families and to be told what to think and do. The population was spared, however; he is now harmlessly selling organic foods in a distant region.

When I say that social workers come equipped with feelings, I do not mean to suggest that we are a horde of ecstatics and gross sentimentalists, or even that we are all neurotics. I simply wish to assert the legitimacy of our feelings. Social workers are often bombarded with stimulation and they need to make their emotions compatible with their reason.

To perform in the job effectively, a social worker must triumph over his prejudices. Those who harbor gross prejudices, extreme racial and sex prejudice for example, are rarely attracted to social work because of the racial and ethnic groups served by the profession. However, bias and personal conflict in the conceptions of human psychology and family-life interaction can be stumbling blocks. Some workers find themselves offering advice to clients when it may really be quite inappropriate for them to do so. They may over-counsel a client before the client is ready to listen — either because the social worker himself is not completely listening to the client or because the worker is responding to something within himself which the client has stimulated. A worker may project onto a client conflicts which are actually his own property. Social workers who habitually "come on strong" to their clients are frequently struggling to express and impose personal biases and conflicts. Clients rarely benefit from such an approach. The old social work maxim continues to be valid: meet the client on his ground, where he is; do not invent conditions which the client does not express.

Of course, it can be exceedingly difficult to maintain equanimity and objectivity, especially when a client is overtly hostile and provocative. At such times, social workers will resort to reflexive ways of protecting themselves psychologically from the hostility. Name calling, accusations and threats of physical injury automatically trigger a worker's defenses.One can use three techniques, or "defensive weapons," when interviewing aggressive clients: a quiet voice, constant eye contact, and a pad of paper. Shouting matches between worker and client are not only unprofessional and discourteous, they will often escalate tensions and constitute a real threat to the worker's physical safety. Loud clients will sometimes quiet down in the presence of a worker who is himself calm, quiet, and at the same time striving to be genuinely communicative. Under these conditions, the client will often seek his own controls. Constant eye contact cannot be overstressed. Inattention will reinforce disruptive behavior. The client needs to know that he is not scaring off his worker.

I have also made it a practice to stress note-taking under these conditions in order to demonstrate my concern for what the client is saying. It can often be essential to let the client know that his concerns are important enough to be written down, so that the worker and client may later examine them together. If this is explained and stressed enough, the client will often adjust his speech to allow the worker time for his notes.

In addition to holding off confrontation with clients and avoiding physical injury, these and other techniques can also be useful in guarding against inappropriate expression of an individual worker's personal conflicts and biases. All of us must recognize the vulnerabilities which make up our individual character; vulnerability, of course, is a valuable and humanizing attribute. But, it should never be allowed to determine the professional response of social workers confronted by manipulative and hostile clients. Unprofessional responses can so permanently shift the focus from the client onto the worker as to make the shift back to the client difficult or impossible. In short, the worker must know himself well enough to be able to select his responses under pressure. He must be able to de-personalize himself to the extent that he is ambivalent to, or disinterested in, his own value system and his own impulses. This can be a Herculean task; on the other hand, there is no equally responsible alternative. Consider the following:

II. *The course of a case*

Sandra was twenty-three years old, black, two hundred and twenty-five pounds. She was frequently intoxicated when arriving for appointments. Her expressed hatred of whites and especially white women was well known to everyone at the office. She had a long series of white women social workers who had successfully pleaded to drop her case. She had threatened the lives of each of them and, on some occasions, to underscore her threats, had thrown chairs and other office equipment at them. In the office, her disruptive and aggressive behavior would accelerate on every attempt to discuss her relationship to her four year old child who had been in foster placement off and on from the time of his birth.[8]

Sandra's case was assigned to me, seemingly as a last ditch effort. I recall my own anxiety and the fear in the faces of the workers who had once carried her case. Nobody thought any progress could be made in developing a therapeutic relationship with Sandra. At this point neither did I. Nevertheless, I was approached by my CSA director and supervisor with the request that I accept the case, because: (1) I was a man; and (2) I was physically strong enough to cope with Sandra's physical aggressions. I would like to think that there was also some recognition of my social work skills. In any event, it was clear to me that many of my co-workers were relieved to have been spared such a case assignment. I had reason to envy them their relief.

With such a formidable task, I found it necessary to ask myself if there were some psychological equipment which I could use that had not been tried before. I decided to focus on two areas; these proved to be vital before any change could take place. First, I confirmed Sandra's intimidating powers. I told her that she had indeed succeeded in scaring off a long line of workers. I could see no value in denying this. Second, I told her that I would not be similarly manipulated.

It did not require special insight to recognize that Sandra enjoyed the fear she stimulated in people. My initial meeting with her in fact had been taken up with listening to her declarations of triumph over social workers. My statements to her could not and did not signify empty posturing. At this point I was fairly certain of what my goals would be in working with her.[9] It was important for me to interpret Sandra's behavior directly since she clearly had the intellectual skills to benefit from non-judgmental interpretation. I gently but firmly persisted in my conviction that her disruptive behavior was masking the terrifying conflicts she felt in her relationship with her child. Any progress would require immense patience and considerable tact since I knew she could at any time reject my attempts for a therapeutic relationship by simply escalating to a point of rage. She had an innate desire to master her own impulses and accordingly I worked to assist her in this without controlling or directing her.

In the course of four months we made exceptional gains. She was finally able to express her highly charged ambivalence — her simultaneous love and anger towards her child. After reaching this milestone, we concentrated on finding ways to meet her special adult needs, in contrast to her child's unquestionable need for a stable and consistent home life. Her child at this stage had been removed from and returned to his mother a total of eighteen times. He was being severely damaged by these events — demonstrating very little language development and showing signs of hyperactivity and chronic anxiety. But, Sandra had come to discriminate between her needs and his needs. That was progress of a kind.

The ground was prepared for the inevitable confrontation. Who would take permanent responsibility for her child? I steeled myself against the anticipated outrage. I advised Sandra of my intention to seek permanent custody of her child. (Her court date was quickly approaching and I had decided that no purpose was served by avoiding the difficult task of what she called 'taking sides'.) "I knew you would say that," was her controlled response.

She did not appear in court for the final disposition on her case — permanent custody was ordered to the Department. She called my office a few days after the Hearing, related that she knew of the judge's decision and that she wished to make an appointment with me for the purpose of signing an Adoption Surrender. The cataclysm did not come. Sandra kept her appointment, signed the Surrender, and expressed her relief that it was finally over.

Sandra's case took its toll on my family. Between milestones there were episodes of disruptive behavior. There had been some of the familiar name-calling directed at me when Sandra and I met at the office. That, I had expected. What I had not expected was her malicious use of the telephone. It was not hard for her to locate my telephone number in the directory. So, late in our relationship, for several weeks she called my home for the purpose of threatening my wife and children. What was I to conclude? At one level my work had simply spilled over into my home life. It is the reason why great numbers of social workers maintain unlisted home telephone numbers. Abusive telephone calls at home, I had come to learn, were a common occurence. Sometimes the job became a twenty-four hour a day ordeal. Nevertheless, it was important not to jeopardize the gains Sandra was making in our work together. It could only have been counterproductive for me to express my dissatisfaction with her practice of making vulgar and threatening telephone calls to my home. It was a side-issue and had nothing actually to do with what she was feeling towards me and my family. There was no reason for me to be personally insulted.

III. *Larger contexts:*

And yet, many people respond personally to disturbed and acting-out clients. Though not limited to this type, it appears to be a special feature of the middle-class white conservative in our culture to be critical of troubled families who receive help from the Welfare Department. Partly, this is because the misery and illness of other people are interpreted as personal affronts. Too many of us hold the view that all persons in American culture were somehow born to favorable circumstances and that the dysfunctional or mentally ill have somehow willed themselves to be sick or disturbed. We may either express or harbor the desire to admonish sick families. We see them as embarrassments and as an unjustifiable drain on our tax dollar. Our fantasy is that by withholding welfare funds and social services the problem will go away or take care of itself. We would have sick families fend for themselves; pull themselves up by their bootstraps!

This perspective constitutes a body of criticism which the social worker hears from the sidelines; it may come from the press, from his own extended family or from the neighborhood. At times, the family social worker feels like a solitary warrior defending his clients, his work, and his profession against the dragon of collective public resentment. He is in an unenviable position. But he cares, and if he cares enough, he endures.

Much of the resentment, I am convinced, stems from deficits in the public's own family-life and mental health education. Sandra was an abusing parent, not surprisingly because she was an abused child. Wordsworth's metaphor illustrates the point: the child is father of the man. Few of us were ever formally taught how to be parents. Our parenting practices are not the result of high school or college study. Accordingly, what we draw on is our own childhoods. In short, we model ourselves after our own parents. When we become parents ourselves, we incorporate our parents' better aspects and reshape or modify their less desirable aspects, each of us doing this according to his own abilities. We also invent new parts.

Abused children, however, have profound difficulty in doing this when they become adults. They are unable objectively to comprehend and evaluate their parents' behavior toward them. They cannot heal themselves. Childhood trauma does not stop exerting its powerful and unrelenting influence to distort the perception of human relations simply because the abused child has come into adulthood. There is no purifying barrier through which any human being moves from adolescence into adulthood which de-activates or removes childhood conflicts. Abused children need psychotherapy and intensive family-life counselling if they are to grow into caring and nurturing parents.

Sensational accounts of child battering and death exist in a number of welfare records. The public is periodically aroused by the reports which reach the press. The public must be aroused, but not for the purpose of retaliating against the abusing parent; people may conclude that he or she is undeserving of any rehabilitative assistance. Also, they must not be aroused for the purpose of retaliating against family social workers who are overworked and who have failed to make the problem go away! Rather, the public must recognize its responsibility to enhance basic understandings of family breakdown; they must advocate the institution of family-life and mental health education in our public schools. Scapegoating serves no useful end. If child abuse is significantly to diminish, it will be because cultural conditions and public education are on the rise. It can also diminish if enough public money and support is directed to existing protective service programs for children. Human service agencies alone, however, cannot do the entire job.

One of the most loathesome conditions of our culture is poverty. Poverty has often been directly responsible for the feelings of anger and inadequacy and states of depression noted in abusive parents. Yet the parents I have counselled did not abuse their children because they were poor. As close as the issues of poverty and child abuse may sometimes be to one another, they are separable. Abusive parents hurt their children because there is something drastically wrong with their mental health. The ability to shut off their aggression or judge the effect of their aggression on their children is out of their control.

Healthy parents have thoughts of harming their children. Whether rich or poor, the healthy parent is able to control his impulses. He knows his limits and can judge the effect of his behavior on his child. What parent has not experienced his own rising aggression and impulse to strike out at a child who is surly, defiant, kicking, and screaming? But, is a parent's reaction determined by his income? I think not, although too often we fall into a trap of equating the two and acting accordingly.

It is a pernicious assertion that poor and abusive parents cannot be helped, or that a family agency should not provide rehabilitative services to them. Our conservative critic will say that such efforts constitute a case of "throwing good money after bad." Our misdirected liberal critic will say that *therapy* for the poor is a sham, a bandaid approach to the problem, and that adequate family *income alone* will solve the problem. While adequate family income has much to recommend it for the purpose of improving the financial condition of poor families, it will not remedy child abuse. Social workers know that child abuse is found in financially solvent families and good mental health is achieved in poor families.

During my term as a family worker I came to be less concerned with the material possessions of the family household as an indicator of family mental health and increasingly concerned with the ability of the parent to discuss his aggression. The inability of the parent to discuss his impulses toward his children was often the best first indicator for suspecting child abuse; and while not all parents who denied having aggressive feelings were child abusers, healthy parents could readily admit that it is difficult enough to be a decent parent to say nothing of the difficulties of vying for sainthood.

VI. Custody and Separation

The Massachusetts Department of Public Welfare retains "custody" of approximately six thousand of the state's children. Custody is a legal term which encompasses (but is not limited to) the right to determine where a child shall live, with whom and under what conditions. (Under most circumstances children are placed directly into a foster home once they have been removed from their natural homes). Guardianship is popularly thought to be a stronger term; actually it is not. In Massachusetts this misunderstanding is partly due to the old administrative misnomer, Division of Child Guardianship, which actually assumed custody, not guardianship of children. Individuals (and corporations) are generally guardians. Administrative agencies are generally custodians. When a judge assigns a guardian to a child, he will have a good idea of what important, yet limited, expectations he wants fulfilled when next he sees the guardian before his court. Most often the guardian is expected to perform the day-to-day duties of the parent — to provide family life, enroll the child in school, take the child to the clinic, and so on. But the guardian is not generally ordered to make major decisions: such as to establish *rules* under which the child may be visited by his biological family: nor does the guardian oversee the range of social, educational, or medical and family services when the child moves out of the guardian's home or neighborhood.

In comparison to guardianship, the following, excerpted from the Massachusetts General Laws, Chapter 119, Section 3 *Definitions* can serve to clarify the meaning of the term "custory":

> "Custody," shall include the following powers:
>
> (1) to determine the child's place of abode, medical care and education: (2) to control visits to the child: (3) to consent to enlistments, marriages and other contracts otherwise requiring parental consent. In the event that the parent or guardian shall object to the carrying out of any power conferred by this paragraph, said parent or guardian may make application to the committing court and said court shall review and make an order on the matter.

Children in the custody of the Department are said to have been "taken into care" — a phrase which merely points up one of several processes which the social worker follows in order to gain custody. Acting as representative of the Department, the social worker will be the specific individual responsible for obtaining custody of a child. Usually the process involves either a "voluntary" agreement with the parent or a formal petition before a Juvenile, District, or Probate court. Voluntary agreements connote a certain measure of cooperation between the parent and social worker; court petitions can connote quasi-adversary proceedings. Often, parents who voluntarily assign custody of their child to the Department are seeking specific services for, or relief from, their child — who may be severely hyperactive, learning-disabled, or emotionally disturbed. Correspondingly, social workers who obtain custody of a child through the courts are often seeking to give relief to the child from a distressful home situation; usually the parents themselves are a major part of the problem. Depending upon one's perspective, the child will appear to be "taken into care" or "taken away." No social worker takes the process lightly. Nobody "snatches" children. The effects of legal proceedings to obtain custody will have long-range impact on the child and family. Every social worker knows this and, accordingly, makes use of the courts as a last resort, when real protection for the child is the paramount issue.

Voluntary custody

There is almost always a measure of distance or detachment operating in a parent who signs a 23sA (Appendix XV). Agreeing to sign the form and allowing your child to be removed from your home is tantamount to saying that something is wrong. It is a difficult decision for the parent and must be respected as such. But, to complicate matters, frequently the parent and social worker may not agree on the nature of the problem at home. The parent's 'message' may be that her child is impossible to live with and is driving her crazy. The social worker may disagree but knows that challenging or confronting the parent at an early stage in their relationship will be counter-productive. The last thing the social worker wants to do is risk alienating a parent who at least is talking with him and saying that "something" is wrong.

Two feelings compete for dominance in the parent who signs the 23sA: a feeling of relief and a feeling of failure. The feeling of relief comes from knowing that the child will be removed from home and, hence, a major source of the parent's irritation will be taken away. The feeling of failure comes from acknowledging incompetence and being unable to "do the job." In short, the parent feels that (s)he has failed at being a parent. The dualism intensifies when the parent addresses the child with the fact that he is going to live with another family or is "going away to a special school." Only the rudiments of foster care or group care are comprehended by the parent, who nevertheless attempts to explain the consequences of the 23sA; commonly the parent is struggling with a conflict in his or her explanation. On the one hand the parent may wish to state positive things to his/her child about foster care while (s)he may be recollecting some "horror stories" (s)he has heard about foster families. On the other hand, the parent may be scaring and threatening the child with these "horror stories" of foster care in order to defend against the feeling that someone else can be a better parent and can do what (s)he is not able to do: "We'll just see how someone else tries to take care of you — then you'll realize that I wasn't so bad after all," or "just wait — you'll see — you can't make it living with any family — nobody can take care of you." The parent in all of this is attempting to salvage some self-esteem, to cope with the feeling of failure and to justify the feeling of relief. Of course, at the same time, the child is being damaged, and the damage will really begin to show when the child physically leaves his home.

Custody through the courts

Child welfare workers make frequent court appearances. A scheduled court day can mean that half or more of the working day will be spent meeting with family members, probation officers, attorneys for the parents, attorneys for the child(ren), an attorney from the Department and other interested parties. These people may be social workers from private agencies who have been asked to submit a third-party report to the court with recommendations for services to the family.

One of the most important times a social worker must attend court is when he initiates a custody action in behalf of a child or group of siblings. This is accomplished by providing both oral and written reports to the Clerk of Courts, thus showing cause why it is in the best interests of the child to take him or her into care. If the Clerk feels that cause is evident, he will arrange a meeting with a judge for an initial hearing. When successful, temporary custody will be awarded to the Department and a continuance hearing scheduled.

Between the time of the initial petition and the first continuance, the social worker will have taken the action which had been the object of his petition, usually removal of the child(ren) from home and placement with a foster family. An independent third party will have conducted a study of the facts in the case — this is usually performed by a social worker from a private social service agency. An attorney will have been assigned by the court to the parents. A separate attorney will have been assigned to the child(ren). An attorney from the Department will have been assigned to the case and will assist the social worker in preparing for the court appearance.

On the morning of the first continuance hearing, all parties in the case will meet and discuss the facts; they will review each other's written reports which will later be submitted to the presiding judge when the case is eventually heard. Areas of conflict and disagreement on the facts and recommendations may be heatedly discussed by the parties at this time. If a consensus can be reached, it will often occur in the corridors, in advance of presentations made before the judge in the courtroom.

During my years as a family worker I made approximately sixty court appearances. Because the Department's legal staff consisted of only a handful of attorneys in the Boston Regional Office — three, as I recall — about one-half of these appearances I made without the assistance of a Department attorney. It was a simple case of overwork. It was common during these years for our attorneys to face each day with a dozen scheduled cases to represent. It was then a matter of course for the attorneys to arrive at the courthouses and discover additional work facing them — for instance, an unexpected encounter with a social worker requesting assistance in presenting an emergency care-and-protection petition was fairly commonplace.

There is no rule of thumb governing a court's handling of a case. Every court has its own character, just as every judge has his own unique style and unique set of expectations. It is therefore important to know something in advance about the court in which you, as social worker, will be appearing. You must know and be ready to conduct several different styles of negotiating, and sometimes, compromising your position on each case. Reasonable compromise on the important questions of placement planning for children, therapy for parents and the projected time of separation of children from their natural families is to be regarded as a successful outcome in court negotiations. Events in court rarely go as the social worker would ideally like them to go. But, for the most part, reasonable compromise arrived at by intelligent and sensitive advocacy among several individuals is in the best interests of the children and their families.

There are sometimes catastrophic exceptions to this process whereby compromise becomes capitulation which becomes failure. In one of my cases a presiding judge ordered me to retain statutory custody of a four year old child and, at the same time ordered that the child be physically removed from his foster home and returned to his own home to live with his mother. The child had been severely beaten by his mother's boyfriend only a few weeks before the judge's decision to reunite the family. The child's mother was only nineteen years of age and very much a child herself. Her dependency upon her abusive boyfriend was quite evident; she shielded him, wished to continue living with him, and minimized the beating her child had received by describing it as a bad spanking. She openly but unconvincingly admonished her boyfriend in front of the judge. This action apparently aided in convincing the judge that she could be trusted to provide for her child's safety at home. The boyfriend attended the hearing as well. The judge also admonished him and asked that he keep his distance from the mother's child.

It was not a major surprise to me that on the day following the child's return to his mother, the mother's boyfriend set fire to her apartment in retaliation for the scolding he had received in court. It was not long after this that this mother and her boyfriend reconciled their differences and began to live together once again. The abused four year old child, of course, had been returned to the same, if not more dangerous, conditions under which he had originally become known to the Department.

Cases like this one do not constitute compromise so much as they constitute a wresting of the casework role from the social worker by the judge. It is this issue which has historically troubled social workers and attorneys within the Department. To what extent should the court take upon itself the responsibility of making casework decisions — i.e., specifying what placements and services will be provided by the responsible social worker for the period the child continues to be the legal responsibility of the Department? It can be a maddening problem when under these circumstances a child is returned to dangerous conditions and the social worker is made powerless to provide for the child's protection.

Another major problem with court-ordered custody is the damage which can result to children when temporary custody fails to result in a permanent custody order to the Department. When temporary custody is continued over periods of years it is impossible for the social worker to develop a stable and permanent plan for a child. During those years the child will have experienced multiple separations from his biological and foster parents. Too often the result is a confused and frightened child who feels that all human relationships are tenuous and impermanent. Conditions like these are almost a certain guarantee that the affected child will require psychotherapy at some point to help him interpret and cope with this period in his life. Such was the fate of Sandra's child who was shuffled between families in the course of five years while the court equivocated on the question of the child's best interests. Most social work professionals, I feel, would support a time limit on the duration of temporary custody, probably one not to exceed one year. The courts, however, will need to look closely at this question and make the necessary improvements where they can in their standards and practices.

Separation is a simple event (removing a child from his family) but a highly painful and complex issue (a child's experience of immense psychological loss). No matter how well prepared to leave his home and family and no matter how undesirable his home and family may appear to an outsider, a child will experience a real and profound grief, not unlike the experience of a child whose parents have divorced. Although the two experiences are not wholly identical, many divorced parents have recognized some of the same symptoms. A child removed from his home hurts beyond comprehension. He may regress, withdraw, strike out, run away, steal or do any number of things to display his grief. He may feel rejected and despised by his parents.

Nothing is familiar in his new setting; he has no sense of belonging anywhere; often he feels that he does not *deserve* to belong anywhere since he may be blaming himself for his rejection from home. His foster mother's house is entirely different from his mother's home: the smells, the food, the furniture, all different. "Nothing is what it ought to be!" Panic! "How do I survive? How can I make the panic go away? What can I do to express my needs?" The older child, capable of some autonomy, who feels lost may actually try to make himself lost in a real sense by running away. A younger child, incapable of sustaining himself on the streets, may openly regress and withdraw, begin to show behavior appropriate for a child much younger than his chronological age.

The child of five to six years may revert to thumb-sucking, soiling his pants, clutching himself, wetting the bed at night. "If growing up means that I will lose my mother, maybe becoming a baby again will bring my mother back;" or, "I am so 'powerful' that I have made my mother go away, making my 'powers' go away will bring her back." There is very clearly a cause-and-effect relationship which must be reckoned with in every separation. It is often the responsibility of the social worker with custody of the child to provide the direct counselling or therapy to the separated child. If the social worker is unable to do this, (s)he will take steps to provide counselling through a community agency. In many cases, however, experienced foster parents are skilled in counselling the children placed in their homes. Foster parents can often make excellent therapists by virtue of their special relationship with the child.

The following is an example of two children grappling with the issue of separation. I think that of all the cases under my supervision, this case has had the greatest impact on me. The children whom I had taken into care were two brothers whom I shall refer to as Joe and William. They were placed in foster homes following a court proceding. Joe, age nine, was bright, out-going and considered himself a "strong" man. Nobody would ever think of calling him Joseph; he was Joe, autonomous and capable. William, age seven, was bright, introspective and presented himself as a "good boy." William was also known as "Junior," but no one would ever call him Bill. Joe exuded self-reliance; William elicited maternal protection. Joe habitually ran away from every foster and group home placement. William eventually settled into one family, but only after he had been 'through' three or four homes. The reason for William's multiple placements was Joe; since the brothers were placed together, Joe's provocative behavior would result in their leaving together. William had done nothing to alienate a foster parent. In the end, despite my belief that they would benefit from being together, experience and wisdom prevailed, and my placement planning for them became geared to meet their separate and individual needs; not to preserve the sanctity of their biological tie.

Joe ran away to be found; William never wanted to be lost. William wanted to recover a "family" as quickly as possible — a family made him feel safe — he spoke critically of his brother for being so badly behaved. William, in short, would mold himself into the quintessentially obedient, tractable child in order to be "loved" and wanted. He manipulated people in a way which he knew would be most acceptable — "I am a good boy, I want to be a good boy for you, I will be cheerful and do everything I am told to do." This was his message to every new adult he met. It was uppermost in his mind at the time of each foster home placement. And this: "I have lost my real mother, yes, but now I will be *your* son."

In coping with the loss of his mother, William had to deny the hurt, to pretend it just wasn't there. It was frightening to acknowledge the hurt feelings. He had to play it safe. He did not feel omnipotent or feel that his behavior had lost him his mother. He probably felt that Joe's behavior had accomplished that. To avoid repeating such a loss, William concentrated on finding ways to make every new environment as protective and predictable as possible. He wore slightly over-sized glasses, carried a book, dressed neatly, and smiled beamishly at all adults. What a safe disguise!

A Painful Case

While William safely coped, Joe was on the run: to quick food diners, car washes, private homes, vacant buildings, abandoned cars, school buildings, and so on. No roots, no security for Joe. Intimacy frightened him. He did, however, endear himself to anonymous adults for short periods and then run from them —

leaving a trail of bewildered people, including numerous foster parents asking themselves and me what they had done to drive him away. To make matters worse, Joe would often take a fistful of cash from these people, thus insuring that his bridges were burned behind him.

Separation and foster home placement did not stimulate any *new* behaviors in Joe; he had a history of running even at the time he was taken into care. These events merely intensified his confusion and self-image as a tough, bad boy. His running away had a two-fold character. It seemed to reinforce the idea in his mind that he was competent and self-reliant, that he could flee from threatening situations; it also meant that he could run home whenever he chose. Running home enabled him to periodically measure the extent to which he felt welcome or unwelcome there. He wanted to be home, but he also knew that home was an intolerable place in which to live. Notwithstanding this, home was home.

Joe's father had been his mother's second husband. Each husband had abandoned the family after only a few years of very unstable family life. His mother was subject to grand mal epileptic seizures, was an alcoholic and had made a practice of sharing her home with groups of alcoholic and severely abusive men. One of these men had made it a practice to enter the bedroom of the children late at night and prance naked about the room, making unintelligible and menacing noises to frighten the children. As a result, Joe and his brother spent many nights barricading themselves in locked closets listening fearfully to brawling noises downstairs where their mother partied with her boyfriends. In the morning the children would find their mother and her guests unconscious on the front room floor, bottles and trash scattered about among pools of vomit, urine and blood.

Joe's step-brother and step-sister, both in their mid-twenties, lived in separate apartments in distant parts of the city. Neither of them wished to take the responsibility of caring for their younger step-brothers. They both worked during the day and could not be expected to provide the close supervision which the children needed, especially Joe. They also feared the consequences of becoming entangled in their mother's problems. However, Joe would often run to his step-sister's house, stay for a few days, steal a neighbor's bicycle or steal from the corner store and be told to leave once again. This sequence occurred often enough so that neither step-sibling could ever become completely uninvolved with Joe.

For a year I chased after Joe. During this time I was constantly pre-occupied with images of him sleeping in alleys and empty buildings, imagining the very real dangers he faced on the streets. I would drive past playgrounds and visit his mother's neighborhood hoping to see him. Touring the streets only rarely worked; most often I would come to learn of Joe's whereabouts by means of a phone call placed to my office by the police or the adult who had most recently taken him in. I am sure that the reason I searched aimlessly for him during many weekends was that I could not bear the waiting and the knowledge that Joe was at risk. Yet, even when I was fortunate enough to find Joe, he greeted me with verbal attacks and physical resistance. His "lashing out" jeopardized all of his adult relationships and, most importantly, his foster home placements.

Nevertheless, after several unsuccessful foster home placements, one finally worked. I was able to place Joe with foster parents who had an unusual tolerance for his rejecting behavior. They would repeatedly accept Joe back into their home after his running and stealing episodes. As a result, his foster parents and I were able to present a united front; our message to Joe was this: "No matter how disruptive and rejecting you choose to be, you have a home to go to and people who care for and love you." We all agreed on the need to break the cycle, break though his fears of intimacy and demonstrate our caring for him over and against his best efforts to fend us off.

Not unexpectedly, our efforts climaxed after one of his running episodes. As usual, upon return to his foster home I carried Joe into the house from my car. Joe was kicking, screaming, swearing and spitting as we went. And, as usual, his foster mother calmly opened the door and led us into the living room. Forty-five minutes passed as I sat on the living room floor holding Joe and protecting myself from his thrashing feet and arms. His foster mother sat on a chair in front of us, speaking calmly and waiting for the tantrum to pass. I thought he would never calm down. Finally he did. I relaxed my grip as he seemed to progressively gain control of himself. Hoping that the worst of the anger had passed, I let him go.

I had misjudged the situation, for when I relaxed my grip Joe leaped from the floor, ran into the kitchen and grabbed a large carving knife from a drawer under the sink. He charged at me with the knife, screaming again with all of the vehemence and anger that had been present when we first arrived at the house. Stabbing me, possibly killing me would be an ultimate form of rejection. I managed to grab his arm and wrest the knife from his hand when he lunged, and, then, without pause, I wrapped my arms around him as before.

Joe's anger had peaked and he began to cry openly; it was the cry of a boy who felt empty, who felt he had nothing left to show for resistance. He felt a terrible relief. His foster mother stood over us and remarked casually that now that the crisis had *finally* passed, we should all sit down and have some tea. We all knew that something very important had just happened. For the first time in my relationship and the foster mother's relationship with him, Joe was able to *begin* to accept and speak genuinely about the feelings which troubled him. Of course this was not a cure. Joe continued to run away and steal, but his severely negative behavior had begun to lessen.

Time and time again his foster parents took him back into their home. But, tragically, personal and health issues affected his foster parents. They were forced to withdraw from the case and, thus, what looked to be a long-term and viable placement had to be given up. At the same time, the Department was engaged in its own administrative Separation. And so, I too, was removed from Joe's life. I was transferred to Assistance Payments on September 5, 1974. Joe was placed at a residential treatment facility in Boston.

While at the treatment facility, arrangements were made for Joe to visit with his mother during weekends and holidays. In April of 1975, in an incident which occurred during one of these home visits, Joe was beaten to death by his step-brother. As the story has been reconstructed, this is believed to have occurred following a dispute in which Joe was accused of stealing money from his step-*sister* whom he briefly visited before he went to stay with his mother. To the best of anyone's knowledge, Joe had not stolen any money and it was later theorized that his step-sister's daughter had removed money from her mother's pocketbook for protection because she knew that one of her mother's friends, a woman with a reputation for stealing, was coming to visit. A short while after Joe's death, the step-sister's daughter explained to her mother that this was, in fact, the case.

Unfortunately, at the time, Joe was accused; and his step-brother was going to teach him a lesson. He removed Joe, screaming and terrified, from his mother's house and brought him to his own apartment. There, it is believed that he removed all of Joe's clothing in order to prevent him from running away, and beat him until he confessed to stealing the money. Joe feigned many confessions and sent his step-brother out on a wild goose chase several times to locate the money. During the step-brother's absences from the apartment, Joe was left behind without his clothes, under his step-sister's supervision in a locked apartment to ensure against his escape. At dawn, after a night of beatings, the step-brother realized that something was wrong. He and his sister lifted Joe onto a couch — Joe, with a broken neck, both arms and legs broken, and few teeth remaining, was dead.

Although I no longer had responsibility for the case, supervisory staff in my office realized my involvement with Joe and his family. Consequently, Joe's assigned worker and I were left with the responsibility of arranging Joe's funeral. We spent long hours with his family and especially with his surviving younger brother, William, reassuring and consoling him. The step-brother, released on personal recognizance at the time of his arraignment, returned to his apartment and lay crying hysterically in bed for two days; he made an unsuccessful attempt at suicide.

The step-brother's suicide attempt came immediately after Joe's assigned social worker and I had visited him. Family members had advised us that William was missing and that the step-brother might have taken him to his apartment. They feared the worst. My co-worker and I went immediately to the step-brother, but William was not there. Another family member, we later learned, had already secreted William away for his protection.

While at the step-brother's apartment, I sat at his bedside while he gave a disjointed explanation of his behavior: He recalled my warning to him a year earlier when he had beaten Joe with a stick. At the time of this incident I had warned him that, as Joe's custodian I would press criminal charges against him if he were ever to strike Joe again. Under no circumstances was he allowed to visit Joe without my authorization. The step-brother had then agreed to my terms; he had satisfied himself that Joe was properly under my supervision and he further agreed that 'punishment' for Joe, if it were *ever* necessary, would come from me and from no one else. Now, after killing Joe, he explained that since I had been "off the case" he had felt justified in taking over the role of Joe's disciplinarian. And since I was not there to "deal with Joe," he would. "Why didn't I listen to you, and why did you have to go away?"

What was I to conclude about the value of Separation? That it was a valuable service delivery model? That it respected the realities of complex child welfare cases? Because the new post-Separation staff found that child welfare work had exceeded their expectations of it, many service worker vacancies became available, enabling me to return to work with the Office of Social Services shortly after Joe's death.

No other case under my supervision has pointed out quite so clearly the violence and vulnerabilities to which the families and children served by the Department are exposed. Added to already overwhelming and inherent difficulties in Joe's case, the interruption of the family casework relationship as a result of Separation, was a disservice with tragic consequences. Likewise, no other case has pointed out to me quite so well the vast responsibilities and areas of physical and psychic injury which are the province of the Department's family social worker.

VII. Conclusions

The family social worker's job is part of a caring profession. His/her feelings cannot be excluded from direct casework and can sometimes serve to enhance the effectiveness of the job (s)he performs. This is the case when the social worker is aware of the psychological defenses which (s)he brings to each difficult experience. It is important neither to deny nor assert those defenses without understanding their presence in us, and making a conscious use of them. It is nearly axiomatic that those workers who deny their own defenses 'burn-out' of their jobs or become jaded and rigid; while workers who live from their defenses sometimes have difficulty distinguishing between their clients' emotional conditions and their own.

The worker is constantly subject to administrative supervision and intervention. This must be so if the agency is to be accountable to the public and the Legislature which created it. The social worker must at every point reconcile those aspects of the job which make him/her a public servant and those which make the worker a unique professional in the social work field. Just as any other professional must, the family social worker must fluctuate between being a teacher and being a student. At one moment the job will require him/her to be a therapist, at the next moment a patient. The worker must counsel clients, and be counselled by supervisors and other specialists in the field.

The Department's family social worker is also accountable to the courts in child welfare and protective service cases. The worker must sometimes uneasily reconcile her-himself to the fact that courts can and do return children repeatedly to their natural families against his/her recommendations. In the case of Sandra's child, as I have indicated, the court equivocated on the matter of the child's permanent custody to the Department over a period of five years, thus making it impossible to develop a permanent plan for the child.

Not only do forces from outside the Department add to the difficulties of developing competent plans for children, the Department, too, will periodically mandate poorly conceived service delivery models. The detrimental effects of Separation, begun in 1974, are still being uncovered, as in the recent and widely publicized case of a child from Somerville, Massachusetts who was allegedly killed by her parents in February, 1978 and whose body was discarded with the trash. A June 26, 1978 investigative report, describing the Department's handling of the case, was distributed to all Social Services staff.[10] One of the 'lessons' of this case is inescapable: Separation has been directly responsible for the mis-management of child welfare cases as a result of the selection and appointment of unskilled and untrained staff to handle them. I have already indicated the role which Separation played in the case of Joe where the immediate and directly ascribable disservice to Joe was the disruption of my established casework relationship with him; the later effects appear to have followed Separation as a tragic matter of course.

One of the most recent of the Department's deleterious service models has been a Protective Service delivery scheme implemented in February, 1978. As structured, the model allows for as many as four distinct social workers to become involved with each family at different points during the supervision of the case, thus, effectively eliminating *any* chance for social workers to become consistent agents of change for any one family. The model fragments child welfare services and may, from my perspective, show the results of its implementation in tragic results to children.

Of course, children in the Department's custody will continue to need homes. We must affirm the value of the majority of foster parents who provide care for the Department's children, and respect the difficulties encountered by our colleagues in Homefinding Units. At the time of my work, each social worker in the Boston Regional Homefinding Unit was responsible for monitoring approximately one hundred existing foster homes in addition to taking responsibility for recruiting and developing new foster placements. They and their foster families worked under constant criticism and hardship, with little or no administrative direction or support from above. Until 1978 there were no uniform policies or procedures for the state's Homefinding Units to follow.

Among all human service agencies in Massachusetts the current emphasis is on the de-institutionalization of children. We want our children in the local community. There is an official projected estimate that twenty thousand reports of child abuse or neglect emanating from the local community will have been received by the Department of Public Welfare during the period July, 1978 through June, 1979. This represents a ten-fold increase over the number of child abuse cases handled during the fiscal year 1975. Can there be any doubt that more front-line family social workers will be needed in the local communities?

With the majority of child abuse and child welfare related referrals to the Department, the inner-city family worker encounters family life conditions in which the entire family's social health and adjustment has been at a low level for many years — sometimes for generations. The statistics covering the expected volume of abuse reports is therefore not surprising. After only two months into the job it was clear to me that the combined attentions of public and private family service agencies in Boston were being directed at a relatively small percentage of the city's population — the tip of the iceberg. Even so, workers' caseloads were consistently high; we provided family crisis work, we "put out fires," we performed a kind of emergency social surgery. Under these conditions, we could do little else. In all aspects of the job, everything to be done tomorrow was supposed to have been accomplished yesterday.

It was my experience, and it has since become part of my general observation, that the Office of Social Services has never been able to provide any truly effective preventive work to many of its families. Its child welfare cases have historically been beyond the point where it has been practical to speak in terms of prevention. The word "prevention" has become part of our human services vocabulary; but, as it relates to the Department's families, it is an idea born out of theory and not rooted in the workers' experience. The concept of prevention, it must be allowed, has considerable merit in treating episodically troubled families. But, when administrators and service delivery model specialists from within the Department have stressed its applicability to the front-line, they have exceeded the limits of an otherwise good idea. At these times, prevention of family dysfunction has been interpreted to stand as a form of administrative 'posturing', and the idea has been sometimes received by direct service staff as a deceit and fraud.

Will the state of Massachusetts significantly increase the number of its direct service staff? History makes this prospect doubtful. Few top-level public administrators have ever advocated reduced social work caseloads. Many Welfare Department administrators in fact favor purchasing direct family services from private community agencies even though these high costs include the cost of the private agencies' overhead expenses. The Department's staff know all too well the practices of private human service agencies to turn away and close out those cases which involve working with the most severely troubled of families. Front-line service staff know that those will inevitably become their families to serve. Nevertheless, if private agency contracts continue to be the trend, and it appears that they will, it is unlikely that the Department will aggressively seek to expand the number of its own social service employees.

As I have stated earlier, the most important element affecting the future of the state's service staff arises from the Legislature's decision in July, 1978 to eliminate the *Office* of Social Services altogether by July, 1979 and to create in its place a *Department* of Social Services. Veteran social workers will most likely continue service with the new Department, despite the problems inherent in coping with such a major transition. Many of us are eager to believe that the new Department will serve as a model to the nation for publically administering social services. Massachusetts has often enjoyed a high reputation among the other states for its position on the cutting-edge of human services legislation and concern for the socially handicapped. There is enthusiasm for what the future holds. Public social work is, after all, immensely important: it is the importance of the work which has kept the individual social worker going.

However, many family social workers are cynical and defeated. At present, too many of us are broadly and justifiably skeptical of the prospects for an entirely new administrative agency. It is difficult to embrace any new enthusiasms. From our position, nearly powerless at the bottom of a complicated human services agency, too many of us feel that we can only surround ourselves with stacks of case records, receive our administrative letters, meet with our clients, struggle with issues affecting our professional development and personal safety, endure, and wait until the next set of "answers" comes.

FOOTNOTES
CHAPTER THREE

[1] In Fiscal Year 1979, The Massachusetts Legislature passed a state budget on July 10, 1978. Since the Fiscal Year had begun on July 1, 1978, the delay resulted in the suspension of paychecks to state employees for a period of two weeks. Welfare recipients were similarly affected.

[2] Legislation to create such an agency was passed by the State Legislature in July, 1978. If the new agency truly materializes, it will be administratively separate from the Department of Public Welfare and may begin operation in July, 1979.

[3] During 1978 the Department employed approximately 2,700 social workers in both Assistance Payments and Social Services. On May 20, 1978, Governor Michael Dukakis stated in a news conference that the Office of Social Services expects to receive 20,000 protective services referrals alone during 1979. The maximum salary for a social worker with seven years' experience with the Department of Public Welfare as of October 1, 1978 is $13,000. The 'burn-out' rate of service workers has traditionally been very high — in many offices there is an annual turn-over rate of 50-80% of staff. Granted, public service employees earn less than workers in the private sectors. But even among public service professional staff, social workers in Boston, for example, earn significantly less than police officers (ca. $15,000+), firefighters (ca. $15,000+), postal employees (ca. $16,000+), school teachers (ca. $16,000+). Postal employees nation-wide have only recently voted down a contract offer which would have raised their median annual salary to a level of $19,000+. According to recent Bureau of Labor Statistics reports, a family of four living in Boston must earn at least $21,000 annually before it can qualify as a middle income family.

[4] Sheehan, David, M., *et. al., The Children's Puzzle: A Study of Services to Children in Massachusetts*, February, 1977, published by the Institute for Governmental Services, University of Massachusetts, Boston, Massachusetts, pp. 16-17.

[5] Sheehan, David, M., *op. cit.,* pp. A1-A2.

[6] In 1973, Massachusetts adopted a child abuse reporting law — M.G.L. Chapter 119, Section 51A — which identified mandatory reporters of child abuse — physicians, social workers, police and other public and private professionals. In 1975, the Department received an average of 43 reports per week: in 1976 an average of 52 reports per week; in 1977, more than 150 reports per week. Latest figures reveal an annual doubling of abuse reports to the Department.

[7] In December, 1977, arrests were made in the Greater Boston vicinity of men involved in such activities.

[8]A psychologically abused and malnourished child, he was frequently rushed to the hospital by his mother when she was afraid of her own impulses to beat him or throw him in front of moving cars.

[9]Namely, to: (1) prepare her to accept a permanent separation from her child: (2) improve her self-concept: (3) counsel her in the area of appropriate adult socialization skills: and (4) provide her child with a permanent foster home/adoption placement.

[10]The report is lengthy (ca. 55 pages) and comprehensive. It explores many issues which are beyond the scope of this chapter to relate here. Many readers, I believe, will recall the basic facts of the case from the extensive media coverage which the case received.

People in our country want others to have welfare benefits but are increasingly resentful about paying the costs.

APPENDICES

APPENDICES

I

Qualifying for
Aid to Families with Dependent Children (A.F.D.C.)

An applicant qualifies for A.F.D.C. if he or she has dependent children who have been deprived of parental support because of death, desertion, illegitimacy, incapacity, divorce, separation, annulment, unemployment of the father, or continued absence of either parent from the home.[1] An applicant and the members of his/her family cannot have more than $1,000 in combined personal property (cash or assets that can be turned into cash, including the cash surrender value[2] of combined life insurance policies). The applicant can own one car, and a house, provided she is living in that house.

A pregnant woman, about to bear her first child, qualifies under the same rules. There are twelve and thirteen year old children in the office applying for aid. If a pregnant woman is under eighteen years of age, and she is already included in her parents' A.F.D.C. budget, she must remain in the budget as a dependent, until she reaches eighteen (or leaves home). If her parents are not on A.F.D.C., she may establish her own budget ($205.70 per month). Her parents will be asked to contribute support, and this support will be deducted from the woman's budget. Pregnant women over eighteen are entitled to their own budgets, and their parents are not obliged to contribute support.

At the time of application, the applicant presents the Intake Worker with two main items. One is her rent receipt, which verifies her residence. The other is a birth certificate for each member of the family. For the moment, this is all that is needed, even if the family recently arrived from another part of the country.[3]

The applicant is the main source of information for the worker. The worker asks questions and the applicant responds. There will be little checking done into other sources to verify the answers, unless they sound too fantastic. If the applicant meets the financial requirements, she qualifies for A.F.D.C. benefits.[4] If she is in immediate need, the worker will issue her a temporary Medicaid card and food stamps.

When accepted into the Program, a mother with three children, with no other income, will receive $357.80 per month. If this mother bears more children, each child will increase her cash grant by about $50 per month (see Figures I & II). Every three months, this family will receive a separate cash payment, the flat grant. In this case, the flat grant will be $113, which is for additional needs like seasonal clothing. Almost all medical and dental needs will be covered by Medicaid.[5]

Figure I
MASS. A.F.D.C. MONTHLY BUDGET FIGURES[1]
Persons Participating in Grant

1	2	3	4	5
205.70	250.80	304.30	357.80	411.20

6	7	8	9	10
464.	518.30	571.80	625.30	678.80

Figure II
STATE BY STATE COMPARISON[1] OF A.F.D.C. WELFARE PAYMENTS

State	Largest Amount Paid[2]	% of Need Standard[3]
Alabama	$148	61
Alaska	$400	100
Arizona	$198	70
Arkansas	$189	65
California	$423	95
Colorado	$290	100
Connecticut	$446	100
Delaware	$287	100
Washington, D.C.	$314	90
Florida	$191	83
Georgia	$141	62
Guam	$300	100
Hawaii	$533	100
Idaho	$344	87
Illinois	$317	100
Indiana	$275	76
Iowa	$369	100
Kansas	$364	100
Kentucky	$235	100
Louisiana	$164	49
Maine	$297	85
Maryland	$254	81
Massachusetts	$385	100
Michigan	$420	100
Minnesota	$404	100
Mississippi	$ 60	24
Missouri	$237	65
Montana	$284	100
Nebraska	$294	89
Nevada	$263	77

New Hampshire	$346	100
New Jersey	$356	100
New Mexico	$220	92
New York	$430	100
North Carolina	$200	100
North Dakota	$370	62
Ohio	$267	62
Oklahoma	$289	100
Oregon	$440	91
Pennsylvania	$373	100
Puerto Rico	$ 54	43
Rhode Island	$359	100
South Carolina	$117	54
South Dakota	$333	100
Tennessee	$139	64
Texas	$140	75
Utah	$352	77
Vermont	$405	76
Virgin Islands	$166	100
Virginia	$311	90
Washington	$416	100
West Virginia	$249	75
Wisconsin	$442	85
Wyoming	$270	100

[1] Any evaluation or comparison of individual state standards should take into account the fact that a state meeting less than full need but having a high need standard may provide a substantially higher level of assistance than a state meeting full need under a lower standard. (This statement and the entire table is taken from H.E.W. Publication No. (SSA) 78-11924, entitled Payment Standards, July 1977.)

[2] Largest Amount Paid is the total payment made to a family of four, with no other income, to meet basic needs.

[3] Need Standard is the amount of money recognized by each state as the level required for meeting basic needs (including shelter) of a family of four. In most states it is this amount against which income from all sources, after application of income allowances and disregard provisions of law, is compared to determine financial eligibility for A.F.D.C. Use of the need standard for determining eligibility for assistance payments is mandatory.

Food stamps are computed on the basis of income vs. certain expenditures (rent, utilities, uncovered medical expenses — like going to a chiropractor, or incurring private school expense). If the above mentioned family pays $225 a month for these expenses, and their only income is from welfare benefits, they will receive $105 worth of food stamps per month. The food stamps cannot be used to purchase paper goods, household items, cigarettes or alcohol. They must must be used solely to purchase food.

An applicant can also be working and apply for aid. She presents the Intake Worker with five wage stubs representing five consecutive pay periods. The worker will allow certain deductions against the gross monthly wages, such as taxes, transportation costs to and from work, day care or babysitting costs, special clothing costs, and a $28 work-related deduction. When these deductions have been made, the remainder is the excess income. If this figure exceeds the monthly cash grant that she would receive from welfare, she is ineligible. If not, she will receive a supplement to her excess income — not to exceed her monthly A.F.D.C. budget — together with other regular welfare benefits.[6]

[1]All rules in this section, and subsequent sections, have been summarized from the Mass. Assistance Payments Manual, Revised 1976, and are subject to revision.

[2]Cash surrender value is the amount of money one would get if she cashed in her policy, based on face value of the policy and on how many years she had been paying on it. For eligibility purposes, the first $1,000 in surrender value is discounted as personal perperty. (Many applicants do not have life insurance, and some are unfamiliar with the concept of life insurance.)

[3]The State has no residency requirements (length of residence) affecting welfare eligibility.

[4]As mentioned earlier, the A.F.D.C. Program is a federal one. The State is reimbursed (about 50-75%) for the A.F.D.C. payments that it makes to recipients, provided that it meets certain Federal standards. Otherwise, each state is allowed to administer the Program as it sees fit, and it is allowed to determine its own benefit levels. These figures are subject to periodic cost of living increases, usually from 3-5%.

[5]Medicaid is the largest part of the Welfare Dept. budget. Medicaid costs for 1978 fiscal year were $626,532,050. By 1980, costs could reach one billion dollars. The principal reasons for the estimated increase are 1) the rise in institutional care costs and 2) a 5% increase per year of people eligible for Medicaid (Medicaid Division, Mass. Dept. of Public Welfare).

[6]There is also a formula applied to wages for those already on welfare and starting to work. This formula, known as the 30 + 1/3 Formula, allows for more deductions against one's wages than the formula used when first applying for aid. It is sometimes more advantageous, then, to wait until after one is receiving welfare to go to work (see section on 30 + 1/3 Formula).

II

A.F.D.C. Applicant's Additional Benefits

In 1974, when an A.F.D.C. applicant was initially accepted on welfare, she could receive various items of furniture and household supplies. In 1975, this policy was discontinued. Presently, she can obtain only a few items. If she does not have a working refrigerator and her landlord verifies that he does not supply one, the Department will give her $308 towards a fourteen cubic foot refrigerator (family of five or more). For families with fewer than five eligible members, the Department provides $224 toward an eleven to twelve cubic foot refrigerator. If her washing machine is broken beyond repair and a repairman verifies this, the woman will receive $236 toward a twelve pound capacity washer, provided that four or more people are in the family. With fewer than four eligible members, the client is out of luck. The Department will pay reasonable costs to repair refrigerators and washing machines.

Both refrigerator and washing machine payments are made directly to the store of the applicant's choice, under the Emergency Assistance Program. An applicant may also receive $150 for moving expenses, under the E.A. Program, if she is in the process of changing apartments.

III

A MONTH'S BUDGET
FOR AN A.F.D.C. CLIENT WITH ONE CHILD
(SEPT. 1977)

ALLOWABLE INCOME		*EXPENSES*	(all items approx. same each month)
Monthly A.F.D.C. Allowance	$243.50	Rent	$176.89
		Gas	$ 5.00
Flat Grant	$ 28.60	Electric	$ 12.00
Salary* (client works as librarian for ecology-oriented organization)	$ 30.00	Phone	$ 10.00
		Food Stamps	$ 29.00
		Food not covered by stamps	$ 30.00
	$302.10	Chiropractor (back problem)	$ 20.00
		School Supplies	$ 2.00
		Plastic Bags (required by landlord for garbage)	$ 1.00
		Train Fare for daughter to school	$ 16.60
			$302.49

EXTRA INCOME,
NOT ALLOWABLE AND NOT
REPORTED TO WORKER

Client receives a varying
amount each month from
sewing, private counseling,
and from her divorced husband.

---

*Clients are not required, by Dept. Policy (Subchapter A, Part 304, Subpart C, Sec. 304.144, Mass. Assistance Payments Manual), to report — for deduction purposes — irregular and infrequent income which cannot be predicted over a period of time, providing it does not exceed $40 per month. Whenever possible, verification of such income is to be made quarterly or more frequently as necessary. Many clients and workers are unaware of the exact amount clients are allowed to receive without reporting it. This is due mainly to workers' unfamiliarity with certain parts of their Manuals.

A MONTH'S BUDGET
FOR AN A.F.D.C. CLIENT WITH ONE CHILD
(SEPT. 1977)

ITEMS PAID FOR WHEN EXTRA INCOME IS AVAILABLE

Vitamins prescribed by chiropractor, needed for maintaining health but not
   covered by Medicaid (approx. $25 worth needed)
Public transportation for client
Dishwashing liquid
Coins for laundromat
Laundry detergent and bleach
Housecleaning and bath soap
Deodorant, toothbrushes, toothpaste, and dental floss
Postage stamps
Writing paper, pens, pencils, envelopes
Books, newspapers and magazines
Aspirin, bandaids, antiseptic, iodine, alcohol and antacid
Towels and sheets
Clothing and shoes
Plastic wrap, paper towels and toilet paper
Feminine hygiene necessities
Shampoo
Scouring powder

IV

The 30 + 1/3 Formula

A.F.D.C. Mothers[1] can work and continue to collect welfare benefits. Once they begin regular employment, they must report their earnings to the Department. A woman does this by presenting five consecutive wage stubs to her worker.

The worker than applies the 30+1/3 Formula to her earnings. The 30+1/3 Formula is known as an 'earnings disregard' and/or a 'work incentive,' because it allows certain deductions against a woman's wages. These deductions allow many recipients to remain on a partial welfare grant whereas, without the deductions, many of them would be ineligible for A.F.D.C.

The 30+1/3 Formula is applied in the following way:[2]

1) Gross wages per week times 4 + 1/3 (average number of weeks in a month over the year)

2) minus $30

3) Remainder of 2) times 2/3

4) Remainder of 3) minus (weekly taxes, union dues times 4 + 1/3)

5) Remainder of 4) minus $28 (work-related expense allowance)

6) Remainder of 5) minus transportation costs to work

7) Remainder of 6) minus babysitting or day care expenses

8) Remainder of 7 is the excess income to be subtracted from client's current A.F.D.C. budget

9) If the excess income is greater than the client's current monthly A.F.D.C. budget, her case will be terminated

10) If the excess income is less, she will receive a supplement to her excess income — not to exceed her current monthly A.F.D.C. budget — plus food stamps, Medicaid benefits, and the flat grant)

When Congress added the 30+1/3 Formula to the Federal welfare laws, it was considered to be a work incentive. Many recipients would be able to work part and full time, and still have some government supplement available to them.

Do recipients consider the 30+1/3 Formula a work incentive?

In the Fall of 1975, four clients were interviewed concerning this matter. They are called A, B, C, and D.

Recipient A worked full time, forty hours per week, at a local hospital primarily concerned with alcoholism and drug rehabilitation. She was a medical secretary and earned $117.25 gross per week. Her take home pay was $99.90. She had two children, ages nine and six, who attended school. She lived in the projects with her children, her mother, and her working sister. Her mother received welfare payments also. Formerly, A worked for Blue Cross as a secretary and for the Afro-American Center.

Recipient A had been 'on aid' since 1970. She applied for A.F.D.C. because she could not keep up with her medical bills. She was twenty-five at the time of the interview, a neat, personable and attractive woman.

In 1975, the standard A.F.D.C. budget for three people was $281.30 per month. By working, A received $432.90 per month net wages, plus a $65.80 A.F.D.C. supplement, totaling $498.70 per month. This came to $5,984.40 for the year. If she had not worked, she would have received $3,375.60.

Recipient A felt that it was worth working, because it gave her a good feeling, and she could not stand to stay home. She liked her job and wanted to get off A.F.D.C. as soon as she could. She said that she did not like the label of handout that is associated with A.F.D.C. recipients.

She stated that if she had worked part time, the 30+1/3 Formula would really have made her think twice about working: she felt that she would not have been able to make enough to get ahead then. A's main concern, however, was medical benefits. She cared more about these benefits for her family than for the money payments.[3]

Recipient B worked part time, fifteen hours a week, as a lunch mother at a local school. She made $3.25 an hour net, totalling $48.75 per week. She had four children and one grandchild living with her. Her twelve year old daughter had recently given birth. Her other children were fifteen, nine, and seven.

B had been on A.F.D.C. for nine years. She was now thirty years old. She applied for aid when she lost her part-time job at Gillette due to illness. Her family was also in need of much medical attention at the time. B had not worked from 1966 to 1973, when she was offered the lunch mother job. She did not work during the school summer vacations.

The standard budget for an A.F.D.C. family of six was $429.70. By working, B received $211.25 in net wages per month, plus a $319.35 A.F.D.C. monthly supplement, totaling $530.60. This came to $6,165.40 for the year. If she had not worked, she would have received $5,156.50.

B felt that she was working for nothing. She thought that the 30+1/3 Formula "took too much of her extra money." Despite this, she stated that she liked working and would not stop. She did not work full time, because she wanted to be home with her children for part of the day. Eventually, she hoped for a better job. The prospects were not good. She had five children, a ninth-grade education, and was fairly unskilled.

Recipient C also had a family of six, but she worked full time at a large corporation. She had been there for three years.

C came to Massachusetts as a Freedom Rider in 1962. She worked at a tailor shop, and did domestic work and laundering at the YWCA. In 1964, her children needed medical attention and she applied for aid. In 1972, she got a job doing assembly line work on a new camera that was being developed. Shortly thereafter she was offered a promotion to work with film developing at one of the company's branch plants. During this time, the Welfare Department paid for a babysitter while C was at work. C had five children, aged seventeen, fifteen, thirteen, ten, and nine. She lived in the projects and paid $99 per month for rent.

C made $186.80 gross per week. She took home $158 but paid $74 per week to her credit union for a car loan. She ended up with $84 per week take home.

The standard A.F.D.C. budget for six people was $429.70 a month. After credit union deductions and application of the 30+1/3 Formula, she had a total monthly income of $420.00 ($60.40 was her A.F.D.C. monthly supplement).

C stated that it was impossible to get ahead. She felt "too honest in reporting her income," and said she should have kept quiet about it, like a lot of people she knew. She felt cheated by the System and by the 30+1/3 Formula, especially since she knew people who were working and collecting full welfare benefits and getting away with it. Despite these feelings, C wanted to continue to work, because it made her feel like she was doing herself and her family good. She also liked her job and her friends at work.

Recipient D worked full time, forty hours a week, for a hotel, doing laundry. She grossed $100 a week and took home $87. She expected to work only until Christmas, because she said it just was not worth it. She attended high school classes at night to earn her diploma. She was twenty-one years old, lived in the projects, and paid $40 per month rent. She had two children, ages three and one.

D had been on aid from 1972. She applied for aid while she was in the tenth grade because she was pregnant. Before applying for welfare, D worked at a hospital, as a dental assistant, at a playground, and at a nursing home.

After D began receiving A.F.D.C., she worked at an egg factory for $1.80 an hour. She said, "It was a dirty place, a real mess. They'd cheat the pants off you, especially if you let them get away with it."

She also worked as a hand presser for a sportswear company. She said, "There was very bad ventilation. The irons were old and coming to pieces. The dust on the floor was so thick, your feet would always get black. Your clothes automatically got dirty."

D's net wages at the hotel were $377 per month, and she received an A.F.D.C. supplement of $96.30, bringing her monthly total to $473.30. This came to $5,678.60 for the year. If she had not worked she would have received $3,375.60.

D wanted to find a decent job, because she did not want her children "to grow up on welfare and be in the same boat." She saw the job situation like this:

"When you grow up, the first thing you say is 'I'm not going to be on welfare. I'm going to make something of myself. I'm going to get a job.' So you go apply for a job. There's a waiting list ahead of you. You go to Unemployment, and there's a list ahead of you. So you're waiting and waiting; months go by, and nothing happens. A couple of places send you a 'Dear John' letter. In the meantime, you're out on your own, grown, and you've got to get your own place, and nothing's happening. So you apply to welfare, just to pay off some of the bills. Because you have to eat, you apply for welfare. You still wait. Welfare comes, you get the check before you get the job. Still nothing happening. Some do get lucky. They get a job and they're able to get off. Others are not. Half the people use welfare as a last alternative. There are some freeloaders, but the majority of people aren't."

D felt that the 30+1/3 Formula was not fair to low wage earners. She wanted to find a better paying, more challenging job, but she realized that it would not be easy.

---

[1] Unemployed fathers may also work and receive welfare supplements. This section, however, is concerned solely with A.F.D.C. mothers, who make up the largest part of a worker's caseload.

[2] 2) & 3), the $30+1/3 deducations, are not allowed to employed A.F.D.C. applicants. The rest of the formula is applied to employed applicants.

[3] Even if a person is not on welfare in Mass. she may be able to obtain Medicaid benefits for her children under twenty-one years of age, provided she meets certain eligibility standards.

V

Fathers in The Home

Families do not always have to break up to qualify for welfare. In certain circumstances, a father may remain in the home while he and his family receive A.F.D.C. benefits.

A family qualifies for aid if the father has worked in at least six quarters of the last 13 (one quarter = a consecutive 3-month period in which a person makes more than $50). Also, the family qualifies if the father has collected unemployment compensation within the last year, and these benefits have expired. The father must be unemployed, or underemployed at the time of application.[1]

The Intake Worker will register the father with the Division of Employment Security, where he will return on a monthly basis to seek employment. The man may also be referred to the Work Experience Program. This State program was established to help unemployed men with families gain employment experience. Those who are referred are required to work three days a week, and to receive job counseling on the other two days. The Program has been controversial because, essentially, it requires that unemployed men work for their welfare benefits.

According to a prominent Union official, "Workfare is a threat to our (workers') livelihood because it forces unemployed fathers on welfare to take jobs at no pay, which would otherwise be available to workers. Even though the current program provides for only thirteen weeks of work for unemployed fathers, any time union work is performed by non-union workers, the effect is a lowering of the prevailing wage rate and loss of negotiating power. Finally, the unemployed fathers who are in the program are forced to work without pay at a job for which they are not trained. During a recession the program could provide a huge pool of free labor to offset any number of layoffs."[2]

Some unemployed fathers are sick and cannot work. They may collect A.F.D.C. benefits for up to a year. If they have not recovered by then, they must apply for permanent disability under the Federal Supplemental Security Income Program. The rest of the family members may remain on A.F.D.C.

Some strikers and seasonal employees, like construction workers and shipbuilders, apply for their families. They receive aid until the season turns their way, or until the strike breaks.

An unmarried couple with children can live together, and the mother can receive A.F.D.C. benefits. Such a case is referred to a Support

Worker (worker in charge of obtaining support money from fathers) who determines if the man can support the family.[3] If the man cannot support because he is disabled or unemployed, his family is eligible for A.F.D.C. (he is not eligible to be included in the budget). If he does not qualify for any other government programs, the woman often stretches her benefits to support him.

A father is not legally responsible for his wife's children by a previous relationship. Therefore, the wife can apply for A.F.D.C. benefits for these children. If she has had two children by another man, she can receive the regular A.F.D.C. budget for two people, $250.80 per month. Food stamps and Medicaid benefits are also available for the children. If her present husband does not earn enough to support her, the woman may also qualify for aid.

Most people registering for welfare benefits are not fathers applying for their families. The majority are mothers who report that the father of their children has deserted the home.

Sometimes a father will remain in the home and the mother will not report it, because it is profitable for him to work while she collects A.F.D.C. Since workers do not make regular visits to clients' homes, these men are relatively safe from detection (unless a neighbor reports them). In some offices, workers are not required to make home visits at all due to work overloads or because some areas are considered too dangerous to visit.

[1]Underemployment, by Department standards, means that the man is working less than 100 hours a month. If he has sufficient work quarters, his wages can be supplemented — not to exceed the family's monthly A.F.D.C. budget. (If the man participates in the Work Experience Program, he may be allowed to work more than 100 hours a month.) These rules also apply to a woman when she is the working member of the intact family.

[2]Edited statement by Union President, Lois Balfour, April, 1978.

[3]The man must also be legally established as the father of the children. Paternity is established (if the couple is unmarried) in adjudication by a court. Or, the man can sign a legally-binding agreement, acknowledging paternity and his obligation to support the children. This procedure is carried out, in part, because of a court decision in Alabama in the 60s. If a man was found in the home by a social worker, he was held responsible for being the provider, whether or not he was the father of the children. The court struck down this procedure, declaring it unconstitutional under the Equal Protection Clause of the Fourteenth Amendment.

VI

Qualifying for General Relief

Single people with no families are eligible for aid. These are the people who apply for General Relief (100% State-run, State-funded benefit program) and who, if accepted, will be known as the G.R.s.[1] They are some of the more destitute individuals a worker sees.

To qualify as a G.R., an applicant must have a medical form filled out by a doctor, stating that he has been disabled for at least 30 days. This disability must prevent him from performing substantial work (20 hours a week or more). This is the main requirement.[2]

Prior to November of 1975, General Relief eligibility was based primarily on economic need. In August of 1975, laws were enacted that greatly curtailed eligibility for G.R. These laws shifted the G.R. eligibility focus from economic need standards to employability standards. As a result, 18,000 single people were cut off the rolls. In addition to these cuts, there were severe cuts in the medical benefits, such as elimination of eyeglasses and false teeth, and hospital care. Some of these cuts have recently been restored.

Some people who apply for General Relief have been stabbed, have hepatitis, or are chronic alcoholics and drug addicts. If a person is disabled but is capable of part-time work, he must live in a residential treatment center in order to qualify for G.R. Occasionally, people cannot apply in person, so a representative of their treatment center applies for them. The checks then go directly to the center in order to pay for the G.R.'s care. One treatment center director did not bother to inform the Department when G.R.s left his center, and their checks continued to arrive for a while.

Some people apply for G.R. because they have a bone fracture. Their disability usually lasts a few months, but their case may be lost in the shuffle when it goes upstairs to the Ongoing Case Worker; therefore, the case may not be reviewed for continued eligibility for six months, or longer.

Less frequently, G.R. applications are received from qualifying people who 1) are full-time students between the ages of sixteen and nineteen, who have not received a high school diploma, 2) are caring for someone who is wholly incapacitated, 3) are residents of halfway houses and are actively participating in a rehabilitation program, 4) have been released from a State school for the retarded or from a State mental hospital, 5) are sixty-five years of age or over, awaiting Federal disability insurance (S.S.I.), or 6) are ex-offenders who have spent at least sixty days in jail, have been out for less than two months, and are seeking work through a recognized State agency (summarized from Mass. Public Assistance Payments Manual, Chap. I, Sec. D and Chap. II, Sec. B).

Some A.F.D.C. recipients may apply for G.R. after their children are overage, no longer in the home, or no longer attending school.[3]

The Ongoing Worker, in the course of other routine work, may notice that a client will become ineligible for A.F.D.C. in a few months, because the children will be overage. In this case, the worker might write the client a short letter, encouraging the person to make new plans shortly. Little else can be done. Most of the time, the worker discovers that the client is already ineligible. In this case, the client is sent an official notice stating that her A.F.D.C. case will be reduced or closed in half a month. Many of these clients are angry and confused, and they feel that they deserve the benefits. They feel that the State has no right to cut them off after so many years.

Men and women in their middle ages come in to apply for G.R. because they have lost their jobs and have run out of unemployment compensation. They cannot qualify if they are healthy, and they are not eligible for any other benefit programs. These are the unlucky people for whom a worker can only go through the motions. They are given a list of employment services like A.B.C.D.[4] (Action for Boston Community Development) or C.E.T.A.; they are counseled for a minute or two; and they are sent on their way, because the Department can no longer help them.[5]

If a person is accepted as a G.R. — after having provided additional documentation, including a rent receipt and birth certificate — he will receive $153.70 per month, if he lives alone. If his rent is over $70 per month (unheated), he will receive another $25 as a rent supplement. The worker often recommends a special diet supplement if his client is too thin, or too fat but, many times, because the client needs the extra money. The most popular, because it is the most expensive, is the high calorie diet, which adds an extra $36.80 per month to the client's budget. To obtain this diet, the client must have a doctor or nurse fill out Form A-22. (Special diets are not available to A.F.D.C. clients.)

Doctors and nurses do not have any qualms about filling out this form. Many of the clients they see are medically underweight or overweight and can benefit from a specific diet, which usually involves eating good, nutritious food. The approval of special diets for G.R.s is a common practice within the Department (see Figure III).

Figure III

SPECIAL DIETS FOR GENERAL RELIEF INDIVIDUALS

TYPE OF DIET	AMOUNT TO BE ADDED
Low Sodium	$18.90
Bland	31.50
High Calorie	36.80
Diabetic #1	27.30
Diabetic #2	29.40
Low Calorie	16.80
Low Fat	15.80

The above types of diets are prescribed for the diagnosis outlined below.

Low Sodium — For treatment of kidney or circulatory diseases such as malignant hypertension, congestive heart failure, nephritis with edema.

Bland — For treatment of peptic ulcers, gastritis, colitis, spastic constipation, diverticulosis or other disorders of the gastrointestinal tract.

High Calorie — For treatment of nephrosis, toxemia, post-operative cases, severe burns, rheumatic fever, tuberculosis, malnutrition and convalescence after illness.

Diabetic — Two diabetic diets are included, varying with the amount of carbohydrates, protein and fat. *No. 1* contains 180 grams carbohydrate, 80 grams protein and 80 grams fat: *No. 2* contains 220 grams carbohydrate, 90 grams protein and 80 grams fat.

Low Calorie — For treatment of obesity.

Low Fat — For treatment of conditions requiring food low in cholesterol.

Unusual diets not listed here shall be treated on an individual basis and computed by a home economist or nutritionist.

A.F.D.C. recipients can share an apartment with someone else and still retain their full budget. Not so with G.R.s. Every different living situation means a change in budget. If a G.R. lives with someone and shares expenses, his grant goes down to $100.30 per month (see Figure IV).

A G.R. receives food stamps and medical benefits. A G.R. food stamp budget usually runs to about $33 worth of food stamps per month. Medical benefits for G.R.s under twenty-one are equivalent to A.F.D.C. benefits. For those G.R.s over twenty-one, medical benefits are more restrictive (since they are 100% State-funded). G.R.s are not covered for inpatient or outpatient hospital services, except for life-sustaining drugs. All other medications are not paid for by Medicaid. G.R.s are in much poorer physical condition than most other recipients, yet they receive the most restrictive amount of covered medical services.

Figure IV
ASSISTANCE GRANTS FOR
G.R. INDIVIDUALS OR G.R. FAMILIES WITHOUT CHILDREN[1]

		G.R.
Group I — *Full Cost of Common Expenses*		
	A. Recipient Living Alone	$153.70
	B. Recipient Living with Another or Others	145.20
Group II — *Sharing Common Expenses*		100.30
	Recipient Living with Another or Others	
Group III — *Boarding*		
	A. Recipient Boarding with Child or Parent	97.20
	B. Recipient Boarding with Other Relative, Non-Relative or in a Commercial Boarding House	121.00
	C. Licensed Rest Homes Personal Needs (Add to the Personal Needs Allowance the per diem rate x 7 days x 4⅓ weeks)	27.20
	D. Licensed Nursing Homes, Chronic Hospitals, Public Medical Institutions, and Intermediate Care Facilities	27.20
	E. Approved Halfway Houses (Massachusetts Association of Halway Houses for Alcoholics)	27.20
Group IV — *No Common Household Expenses*		
	G.R. recipient not responsible for household expenses	55.60

[1]G.R. families without children are treated as separate individuals, for budgeting purposes.

[1]Among workers, G.R. is a shorthand reference for General Relief recipients, and will be used as such for the remainder of this section.

[2]The financial test of eligibility requires a G.R. to have $250 or less in cash or liquid assets. A G.R. can own a car, and a home, if he lives there.

[3]Children are eligible for A.F.D.C. until they turn twenty-one, if they are still in school, even if they are away from home. A child is cut from a budget if she is sixteen and not attending school, or not registered for the W.I.N. Program (Work Incentive Program). If the child is registered for W.I.N., she can remain in the budget until she reaches eighteen.

[4]Both A.B.C.D. and C.E.T.A. are separate programs not administered by the Welfare Department.

[5]A recent Department policy has established a new General Relief eligibility category. General Relief applicants who are forty-five years of age or older, and have "significant barriers to employability as assessed by the Division of Employment Security" are eligible for General Relief benefits.

VII

Qualifying for
Aid to Cuban, Vietnamese and Cambodian Refugees

There are a few single people who are candidates for the Cuban, Vietnamese and Cambodian Refugee Programs. The Programs were established by the Federal government to help refugees after the Vietnam War and the Cuban revolution.

If the applicant is in need[1] and brings his immigration card, rent receipt and social security card to the office, he can become a recipient with this special status. The applicant does not have to be disabled to qualify.

These people will benefit more than the G.R.s. They will receive an A.F.D.C. budget of $205.70 (one person) per month, and a flat grant of $43.20 every three months. They will receive complete A.F.D.C. medical benefits. They can also receive aid while attending college.[2]

Cuban, Vietnamese and Cambodian families are also entitled to regular A.F.D.C. benefits under these special programs.

---

[1]The financial test of eligibility for these people is the same as for A.F.D.C. applicants.

[2]A.F.D.C. recipients may also receive aid while attending school or college. G.R. recipients cannot receive aid while attending college. The Welfare Dept. does not pay for any client's school or college tuition. However, the Dept. will pay for an A.F.D.C. client's books (for a college course, high school diploma, or training program) up to $100 a year. The Dept. will also allow a basic allowance of $2 per day, or up to $20 per week, if warranted, for lunch and public transportation (for a 2-year period). The Ongoing Worker is responsible for reviewing eligibility for these payments, for verifying the days of school attended each month, and for processing the payments.

VIII

The Intake Process: Workers and Applicants

Each Intake Worker has about 15 applicant appointments scheduled for the week. About ⅔ of them will keep their appointments. Some of them return day after day to bring in the required verifications or to gripe about the process. Then there are the people from last week and the week before. Since the unit is on the first floor, some people come right into the office, interrupting work. Between 9:00 a.m. and noon, a worker sees about five applicants, often with their friends and children.

The worker concentrates on getting the 12-page A.F.D.C. application form — the AP-1 —done, with the fewest number of problems and in the shortest time (the G.R. application form is four pages long). The Department recently revised the AP-1 in an effort to consolidate material for more efficient use.

The revision of forms affects many people within the Department. Forms are the lifeblood of the system. Workers spend a lot of time filling them out and, by necessity, thinking of ways to cut corners on them. Therefore, a revised form which makes things easier is welcomed by the workers.

To an administrator in the system, a revised form may mean new life for her particular program. In 1976, a program called Project Good Health began. The purpose of the Program was and still is to introduce clients to the preventive aspects of health care and to the medical services available to their families. Intake Workers were told to help their clients fill out a two-sided form that would be used to determine the family's health needs. The PGH-21 became one of the many extra forms needed to complete the application process.

Workers usually establish a forty-five minute time limit for taking an A.F.D.C. application. In a busy office, workers are in a hurry to complete their interviews. All of the forms connected with the application must be completed. Some forms are difficult to explain to the applicant, especially if the applicant does not speak English. Other forms are left to the end of the process, when both worker and applicant are bleary-eyed and worn from the parade of papers. Thus, a worker often says: "This form is not important, just sign on this line."

The PGH-21 was such a luckless form. Most workers left it for last and gave it superficial treatment. However, when the AP-1 was revised, the Project Good Health form was incorporated into page two of the new application. P.G.H. administrators were overjoyed with the advantageous location on the main form. They felt that workers might get the message that Project Good Health deserved the attention a page two position demanded. After all, the form is the message.

During the application process, a detachment is established between worker and applicant. The worker strives to go by the rules, asking only the necessary questions. All very official — and dull. Yet, for efficiency's sake, it is better to remain uninvolved with the applicant. It is not the worker's job to become interested in the applicant's life.

When the application has been taken and the necessary verifications are received, the worker visits the applicant's home in order to verify residence. He first looks for the name on the mailbox. He makes sure that the person lives here, that he has not been given a fictitious address. (Workers rarely, if ever, make a second visit to a client's home. Practically all business is done in the office.) Upon entering the house, the worker looks around, but not too suspiciously. This woman has a studio apartment with only one bed. She has two children. How does she do it? The question is usually not asked. It is enough that she lives here. Rarely is anything asked which is not required information.

Occasionally, situations are very illogical. A G.R. applicant will come in with a $300 rent receipt, and he will be applying for a $178.70 budget per month. Or an A.F.D.C. applicant with $415 in subsistence expenses will apply to receive a budget that will give her $411.20 per month. Each of these applicants will be accepted, if all proper verifications are presented (the client may state that his present situation will soon change). The worker recommends that these cases be watched closely when they go to the Ongoing Unit. However, there is a good chance that the cases will be lost in the shuffle when they are sent upstairs.

IX

The Emergency Assistance Program

Emergency Assistance is an optional Federal program administered by the Department. The Federal government reimburses the Department at the rate of 50% for payments made under E.A. "E.A. was enacted in 1967 to provide families[1] with certain payments, medical or remedial care, or other services 'necessary to avoid destitution of a needy child' or 'to provide living arrangements in a home for a needy child' (42 U.S.C. §606(e)). Congress realized that families would need another way of obtaining certain items in disaster, hardship, and emergency situations, instead of using their already strained budgets."

"A.F.D.C. recipients are eligible for E.A., unless 1) 'the necessity for E.A. arises because the child, parent or caretaker refuses, without good cause, to accept employment or training for employment,' or 2) 'the needy child and his/her family has available resources' (these limitations are embodied in 42 U.S.C. §606(e))."[2] Clients' applications are limited to any thirty days in a twelve-month period. Once the client applies and is accepted for E.A., she has thirty days in which to make any additional E.A. requests. When the thirty day period expires, E.A. benefits cannot be granted for another year.

"There is a genuine need for the E.A. Program,[3] and there are three main groups who use it: 1) victims of natural disasters or other destructive acts which are beyond the control of the family, 2) recipients who mismanage their basic monthly grants, and 3) people living in financially unrealistic living situations."[4]

Under E.A., a client may obtain a refrigerator or a washer (explained previously). If a client falls behind on her utility bills, the Department will pay gas and electric arrearages for any six months chosen by the client, provided that the utility company supplies a month-by-month breakdown of the bill.[5]

Oil arrearages will also be paid for up to six months. Rent arrearages are paid for any four months that the client chooses. If a client owes more than four months' rent, her social worker will put her on 'protective rent.' This means that her rent, plus a small sum (to pay the outstanding arrearage), is deducted from her budget every month and sent directly to her landlord, until the arrearage is paid.

In 1977 and 1978, a Federally-funded program, administered by a local agency, provided help with utility and heating bills beyond the provisions of the E.A. Program. Payments of up to $250 were made available to qualified elderly and needy families, including A.F.D.C. families. One of the qualifications for A.F.D.C. recipients was that they had to have exhausted their E.A. benefits for the year.

The local agency did not distinguish between estimated and actual readings of utility or rental bills. One recipient's heating bill of over $150 was paid by the Department under E.A.; then, about a month later, she received another estimated heating bill for a one-week period (in July) totaling over $200. She applied for the special Federal assistance, and the estimated amount was paid.[6]

The utility companies have a large stake in programs such as E.A. and the special Federal assistance programs (utility companies in the area did extensive mailings and press releases to inform people of the special Federal program). Many bills would go uncollected if it were not for Welfare Department payments.

Under E.A., a client may also receive 1) $150 in inner-state moving expenses;[7] 2) a bed and mattress for a child in the home, no earlier than three months before nor later than three months after the child's third birthday, 3) storage payments for furniture, when the storage costs total less than the cost of new furniture, 4) payments for temporary or emergency living arrangements in hotels or motels when no other arrangements are available, and 5) home repair costs of up to $500, when living conditions are detrimental to the health and safety of the family. (When a baby is born, the client is given $125 — $50 to pay for a layette, and the remaining $75 to buy a crib and mattress. The crib and mattress payment had been included under E.A., but it is now a separate benefit.)

In the case of a natural disaster such as a fire, flood, hurricane, tornado, or earthquake, or, in the case of a fire or flood not caused by nature but beyond the control of the family, E.A. will provide 1) one month's rent in advance if the family must move, 2) basic furniture in accordance with policy standards, 3) food and clothing in accordance with policy standards, 4) moving expenses of $150, and 5) de-odorization of any smoke-damaged furniture, and dry cleaning of clothing (summarized from Mass. Public Assistance Payments Manual, Chap. IV, Sec. A, Part 4, Page 1). In the case of fire, the client must bring in a report from the Fire Department which lists the damaged items and/or the extent of damage to the apartment. The social worker may have to visit the apartment to verify the report, but this is rarely done.

To obtain certain items under E.A., the client must go to a store where she will select the items for which she is eligible. The store will give her a written estimate of the cost which she must present to her worker, who will review and process it[8] (see Figures V, VI and VII). E.A. is an active program used frequently by clients.

Figure V

ONE MONTH'S EMERGENCY ASSISTANCE EXPENDITURES
AT A LOCAL OFFICE*

ITEM	AMOUNT DEPT. ALLOWS PER ITEM		TOTAL
13 movings	$150		$1,950
11 beds	$130		$1,430
1 kitchen table and 4 chairs	$107		$ 107
2 dressers	$ 89		$ 178
3 general household supplies	$ 68	for each of the first 2 eligible family members, and	$ 389
	$ 23	for each add. family member	
4 washers	$236		$ 944
1 washer repair (any reasonable repair cost is accepted	$ 92.50		$92.50
1 food supply	$ 34.50	per mo. for each indiv (fig. div. by no. of days of emergency need)	$62.40
2 12 cu. ft. refrig.	$224	(under 5 in fam.)	$ 448
9 electric arrearages	— amount for any 6-mo. period		$1744.50
4 oil arrearages	— amount for any 6-mo. period		$1781.30
12 gas arrearages	— amount for any 6-mo. period		$3099.70
6 rent arrearages	— amount for any 4-mo. period		$4301.35
			$16,349.75

*Approximate costs for the E.A. Program for Fiscal Year 1978 were 12.9 million, the State paying one half and the Federal government paying one half. (Welfare Dept., Div. of Budget). Total expend. for the A.F.D.C. and G.R. prog. in FY 1978 was $524,332,065, not includ. Medicaid payments (Welfare Dep., Div. of Research and Planning).

Figure VI
EMERGENCY ASSISTANCE
STANDARDS FOR CLOTHING
Schedule B
Adult

FEMALE	AMOUNT ALLOWED
2 Dresses	$16.40 (each)
1 shoes	$12.20
1 Sweater	$11.00
1 Winter Coat*	$31.70
1 Boots₁	$ 9.80
1 Sweater*	$10.70
Basic Underwear Supply	$18.40

MALE	AMOUNT ALLOWED
2 Shirts	$ 5.10 (each)
2 Slacks	$12.30 (each)
1 Shoes	$15.30
1 Sweater	$10.00
1 Winter Coat₁	$31.30
1 Boots₁	$10.00
1 Sweater₁	$10.00
Basic Underwear Supply	$14.50

*These items are to be provided for winter months only.

Figure VII
EMERGENCY ASSISTANCE
STANDARDS FOR CLOTHING
Schedule C
Child*

GIRLS	AMOUNT ALLOWED (Under 7 yrs.)	AMOUNT ALLOWED (7-12 yrs.)
2 Dresses	$12.00 (each)	$17.70 (each)
1 Shoes	$10.10	$13.30
1 Sweater	$ 6.40	$11.20
1 Winter Coat*	$25.30	$30.70
1 Boots*	$ 8.20	$ 8.60
1 Sweater*	$ 6.40	$ 8.20
BOYS		
2 Shirts	$ 4.50 (each)	$ 5.20 (each)
2 Slacks	$ 7.50 (each)	$13.30 (each)
1 Shoes	$11.50	$14.50
1 Sweater	$ 6.40	$ 8.30
1 Winter Coat**	$23.90	$27.90
1Boots*	$ 8.20	$ 9.70
1 Sweater*	$ 6.40	$ 9.80

*Clothing for children 13 and older is to be provided in accordance with Schedule B.
**These items are to be provided for Winter months only.

[1] This includes A.F.D.C. families, and families who are not on welfare, if they meet certain eligibility requirements. G.R.s are eligible for limited E.A. payments (in cases of fire or other natural disaster, a G.R. may receive food, clothing, and an advance month's rent if a move is necessary).

[2] Quotes originally appeared in Kevin Malley's unpublished graduate school paper, "Budgeting for Emergency Assistance: The Massachusetts Experience," p. 4.

[3] An Office of Research and Planning survey, entitled "The Emergency Assistance Program," covering the period of September 1975 through October 1976, revealed the following: during the period, at least 1,200 families had their gas shut off because of non-payment of bills; another 750 had their heat shut off; 750 could not afford oil; and 850 were evicted or had their mortgage foreclosed. Most of the utility shutoffs lasted only a week, although a few lasted considerably longer (this material presented on page 18 of "Budgeting for Emergency Assistance: The Massachusetts Experience," by Kevin Malley).

[4] Kevin Malley, "Budgeting for Emergency Assistance: The Massachusetts Experience," p. 20.

[5] Sometimes, a company incorrectly itemizes two months' bills into one month; thus, a six-month statement might actually contain eight to 12 months' worth of bills.

[6] Estimated utility bills are sometimes used by workers in figuring a client's monthly expenditures for food stamp budgeting purposes. Since these estimates usually exceed actual costs, food stamp allotments are usually larger when estimated bills are used.

[7] A.F.D.C. families who decide to move out of State are eligible, under certain circumstances, to receive bus fare for all family members to their new location (under the Transportation Assistance Plan).

[8] The cost of the items on the estimate must match exactly the amount the Dept. allows for each item. This is why many furniture stores which serve welfare customers charge amounts exactly aligned with Dept. price guidelines. When the Dept. raises its allowances, a store raises its prices to match.

X

Overpayments and Fraud

Most clients have worked at one time or another to bring in extra money. Sometimes the amount is so small that they are not required to report it. Some take a chance and do not report larger wage amounts or amounts received from other sources, like Social Security or support payments. If the wages or payments are untaxed and free from red tape, like tips, babysitting, sewing, or typing, the client will probably escape detection.

The client's chance of getting caught increases if the extra income is from another governmental source. The Department runs computer crosschecks with various agencies, such as the Department of Employment Security and Social Security. The worker, after receiving a printout of the clients receiving other benefits, is required to notify each client that this benefit amount will be deducted from the budget each month hence.

Every so often, a worker will receive an anonymous letter or phone call, informing on a client who is working or who has a man in the home. The worker will follow up if he has the time and/or the inclination. Also, if the client fails to keep office appointments or is consistently absent from the home when the worker calls, the worker may become suspicious.

In situations where an overpayment is made to a client, either because of a mistake by the Department or by the client, or because the client deliberately failed to report a change in income, the worker has three options: 1) ignore the entire affair, 2) press the client for recoupment of the money, or 3) refer the case to the Bureau of Welfare Auditing for an investigation (steps 2 and 3 may be carried out simultaneously).

Despite the forms and the time involved, workers usually follow through on discovered overpayments unless the overpayments are very small.

The Bureau of Welfare Auditing[1] is charged with the responsibility of investigating fraud on the part of recipients and vendors (providers of both medical and non-medical goods and services to recipients). The Bureau also investigates check fraud (the stealing of recipients' checks from their mailboxes) and State employee fraud, such as 1) State workers who do not turn over monies paid to the State, 2) workers employed by the State who illegally collect Welfare benefits, and 3) State employees who steal checks from the computer room.

The Bureau works with the Department of Agriculture on food stamp fraud in cases where food stamps are stolen from mailboxes, or where blank coupons are stolen and altered.

Since 1972, the Bureau has received between 3,000 and 5,000 fraud referrals yearly. Workers, when they suspect fraud, make a fraud referral and send it to the Regional Office to be routed to a Bureau investigator. Reports on these referrals are made to the Attorney General and then to the District Attorney. Amounts over $10,000 involve the Attorney General and the Superior Court (mostly vendor fraud).

A typical fraud case involving a client follows: The client had worked for a year without reporting it, because her boyfriend assured her it would be all right. Somehow (probably through a computer check with Unemployment), a Welfare investigator discovered her. She had made $2,700. The investigator called her into the office in an effort to settle out of court.

She agreed to pay $20 a month from her A.F.D.C. budget, in restitution. Before the month was out, she requested that her case be closed, and she moved out of the State.

One Bureau Investigator says:

"Recipient fraud, which usually runs between $1,000 and $7,000, is resolved at the District Court level. One problem with recipient fraud is that the courts are too lenient. The attitude is 'how are you going to get money from a person who doesn't have it.' A larger problem is that the System, as it is set up, allows for fraud. The Department should get the big companies to print out sheets of employees. There should be harsher restrictions on entering the System, like residency requirements, and closer investigation at Intake. More explanations of rights should be given to applicants, so that they know that they can work legally and still be on welfare."

"Instead of requiring harsh jail sentences, stricter repayment plans should be enforced. And more staff should be hired for the recoupment process, since it is now failing in many local offices, due to lack of people to tend to the paperwork."

"Fraudulent clients should not be allowed to go back on aid for a time, after they have been prosecuted. The only justified fraud is when people work for extra money, just to get by."

"Things are different today. Years ago, a client could not have a telephone or a car, or a man's suit in the closet. The worker came every month and checked under the bed for extra shoes. Clients were afraid of their workers then. Now they come into the office, and they want to beat their workers up."

Many of the fraud referrals, and the ones involving the greatest amount of money, involve vendors. Doctors' and dentists' cases often run between $50,000 and $100,000.[2] The fraud often consists of billing for medical or dental services which have not been performed. An ambulance company may bill Medicaid for delivering clients to the hospital, yet the service had never occurred. Instead, the driver may have entered the out-patient clinic of a hospital, secured the names and social security numbers of people who were in that day and claimed them in his billing to the Department. A nursing home might overcharge a Medicaid patient. A pharmacist might fill a prescription for 100 pills by splitting the order into two 50-pill prescriptions, so that he can collect the Medicaid processing fee twice.

Medicaid fraud is a widespread problem occurring in many states. A reporter for a Philadelphia newspaper, Hoag Levin, did a series of reports on the problem in his city. He uncovered a network of unethical drug dispensing headed by doctors known as "croakers."

These doctors would often have very small offices in welfare neighborhoods. All day long they would dispense highly sought after drugs, like valium and other depressants and stimulants, to Medicaid patients. Mr. Levin went to one such doctor who had an office the size of a broom closet. The reporter had been able to secure a false Medicaid I.D. card easily. The names of these "croakers" were passed around on the street, so he knew where to find the office.

He presented his I.D. card to the doctor and told him what he wanted. The doctor would either dispense the drug or write a prescription for it. The entire process took less than 5 minutes. The doctor would then bill Medicaid the standard fee for examining this "patient."

Levin reported that many of these doctors were making a million dollars a year. He also commented on the ease with which food stamps could be illegally obtained.

---

[1] The Bureau is known by many in the Department as the Fraud Squad.

[2] Three local dentists had their licenses suspended for six months to a year, for allowing dental assistants and non-registered dentists to practice dentistry on some of their patients. The first dentist had collected $441,000, the second had collected $328,000, and the third, $501,754. All monies were collected from Medicaid for a one-year period (*Boston Globe* 1977 news story).

XI

General Working Conditions

For years, working conditions in many of the local offices have been a source of friction between workers and the administration.

In 1974, the situation came to a head with the filing of a grievance on behalf of the eleven local offices in the Region. The grievance stated that the Department had violated the following provisions of the Union Contract: Article VIII — Physical Plant Facilities, Supplies and Equipment. The first section of this provision stated that "the Department agrees to provide for all employees adequate, clean, well-ventilated, well-lighted, safe and sanitary office space." The other two sections involve adequate interviewing and conference areas, and working equipment and supplies (adequate telephones, forms, Manuals, etc.).

Union grievances must go through several steps. In the initial steps, Department administrators must answer the complaints. If they agree to the terms of the grievance, the matter is resolved at this level. If not, the final decision lies with an independent arbitrator.

In the first few steps of this grievance, Department officials found no violations of the Contract. One administrator stated in his answer, at the Step 3 hearing: "Some of the problems identified in this grievance are manageable and are being addressed, and others are not so manageable for a variety of reasons. As an arbitrator pointed out in another case, 'Nobody can expect an old building to be free of physical problems, and we are talking here, mostly about old buildings.' As the arbitrator also pointed out, 'If social workers are to be located where they are readily available to their clients — and they want this — they must, and do, accept the fact that they are going to have to settle for something less than first-class quarters.' This citation by no means is intended to make light of or to otherwise rationalize the physical and logistical problems existing throughout the Region'."

The administrator ended: "I conclude that the Department is making efforts to the extent that I cannot reasonably find the Department in violation of Article VIII" (the decision was rendered in January of 1975. The grievance was originally filed in July of 1974).

The Union then brought the matter to Arbitration. The arbitrator and representatives of the parties toured the local offices in July of 1975 (evidence revealed that all of the local offices were leased, either from a private landlord or from the City and that the Department was a tenant at will [no lease] in most of the offices).

A summary of the arbitrator's findings follows: "1) it is readily apparent that violations of Article VIII not only exist, but are quite prevalent, 2) there is a continuous shortage of supplies, and although repeated requests are made to Central Office nothing is done to remedy the problem, 3) many of the offices have woefully inadequate telephone equipment, 4) perhaps the most serious problems is the total inadequacy of space available to members of the bargaining unit (workers), such as four, five and six employees crowded in one room, 5) alarm systems are needed in offices that do not have them, in order to prevent the theft of both personal and Department property, 6) in general, most offices can not be considered 'clean and sanitary' as required by Article VIII, 1a. Walls are dirty and in need of painting; windows are broken and dirty; ventilation is inadequate (unbearably hot in the summer months); bathrooms are unsanitary; cockroaches are commonplace; heating is erratic; lighting is generally inadequate; when supplied, venetian blinds are filthy; window screens are lacking; electrical wires are exposed; radiators are leaking; ceilings are peeling, and 7) these violations constitute conditions obviously within Department control and readily correctable with a minimum of financial expenditure. They were caused primarily by inattention and neglect.[1]

The arbitrator suggested certain corrective actions, and some of the situations have been remedied. Telephone equipment and general office supplies are more adequate, and more security has been implemented at some of the offices.

Yet many of the problems still persist, and the Department is slow to act.[2] The problems of neglect are not limited to this Region. On Friday, February 25, 1977, toilets overflowed at a suburban office,[3] spilling sewage and water throughout the basement working quarters. The following Tuesday, Union representatives visited the office because workers had complained about the slowness of cleanup operations. They found "the basement rugs thoroughly soaked, water stains on the first floor ceiling, and an unpleasant odor pervading most of the building."

On the following day a Department representative met with workers and Union representatives, and on Thursday, March 3, the workers in the basement were moved to different quarters. The workers wanted the entire office staff moved to new quarters, because the overflow was an ongoing problem; but there was some disagreement on the leasing arrangements in this location, and action was stalled.[4]

There are Federal Occupational Safety and Health Standards which exist, but they are consistently overlooked. State employees' recommendations often go unheeded, and there is no effective mechanism to ensure strict enforcement. Health and safety problems are left for workers and their Unions to solve with their respective Departments.

Physical and psychological working conditions have also deteriorated in certain offices because of 1) the decline of the general area due to economic conditions, and 2) the increasing adversary role between client and worker in recent years. Worker discontent and bitterness have been passed on to clients.

Some offices are more perilous than others, especially in the economically depressed sections of the city. Trouble often comes in cycles, and it usually involves purse snatchings, office break-ins, and client assault against workers. When people break into the office, they steal typewriters, radios, blank food stamp coupons and grocery orders. Sometimes, they try to steal the copying machines. If they are malicious, they break windows and other items.

One office had a particularly bad time. The office is in a very run-down section of the city. This incident started with a hold-up. A worker was parked on a side street, one block from the office. He was getting into his car when he waved to someone he thought he recognized. A man approached the car and asked the worker for directions to a street that was on the next block. The man then said, "Hey man, want to buy a .38?" The worker said no and began to turn the ignition key.

"Don't turn that key or I'll blow you away."

The worker then noticed something under the man's shirt, and the man demanded money. The worker gave up his $11, and the man took off down the street.

In another incident, a few days later, a worker was walking along the sidewalk in front of the office. Someone ran by and grabbed her pocketbook. It would not come free. It was tangled around her arm. She was dragged along the pavement until the purse came loose (the worker was later transferred to another office). Soon after that, an employee's car was broken into, and some items were taken from the glove compartment.

The next incident occurred in the office. A G.R. came in to get emergency food stamps because his stamps had not arrived that month. The caseworker discovered that the G.R. had described the same event for three or four months in succession, so he decided to check out the situation. He told the G.R. that he would have to wait for the stamps until the problem could be identified. The G.R. struck the worker. A supervisor came in, and the client began pulling his shirt. A wrestling match on the floor resulted. The police were finally called by the security guards, and four of them took the G.R. away.

A day or two later, a few workers were looking out their windows when they noticed that one of the workers' cars was on fire. The fire department was called, but the car was destroyed. It was discovered that oil had been poured over it and set afire. No one knew the reason (this worker was later transferred to another office).

On Friday of the same week, a G.R. came into the office to inquire about his case. The case had been closed because he was collecting benefits in two offices. He also wanted to learn about the emergency benefits he had applied for — he had been burned out of his apartment. He was referred to an administrator at this point, because he had become agitated. The administrator explained that the fire report was received, but that the report stated only $50 of damage was done. According to the report, the client did not lose anything in the fire. On hearing this, the G.R. spit in the administrator's face. The security guards were called and the man was taken away.

A meeting was held in the office the same day to discuss security measures. Staff decided to request two additional security guards and to request that the Department meet with the Police Commissioner to obtain more police surveillance of the area.

The following Tuesday, a worker was getting out of his car in the parking lot. A well-dressed man, carrying a briefcase, came over to her and asked her for a match. She said she did not have one, so the man said he would have to take her pocketbook instead. He grabbed it and walked off.

Later in the week, a man came into the office asking for food stamps. While he was waiting, he suddenly dropped his pants in front of the worker, only to reveal another pair of pants underneath. The worker chose not to respond to his strange behavior. She determined that he was ineligible for food stamps. She denied his request. He promptly threatened to kill her. The police were called, they removed him from the office but they did not arrest him. He returned to the office near closing time and caused a disturbance. The security guards called the police again, who handcuffed the man and took him away.

The office has quieted down considerably since then. Four security guards were hired, and the police occasionally park in front of the building during the morning.

<hr>

[1]Arbitration Case No. 1139-1164-74, Service Employees International Union, Local 509, A.F.L.-C.I.O. and Massachusetts Department of Public Welfare, October 31, 1975.

[2]The Union has periodically tried to have the Dept. satisfactorily resolve the aforementioned grievance. However, in the new three-year Union Contract, signed in 1977, a clause was written in that prohibits workers from bringing grievances concerning building conditions to Arbitration. The Dept. therefore feels that the aforementioned grievance is no longer valid. The Union has argued that it is, since the Arbitrator in the case kept jurisdiction over the case in order to insure compliance from the Dept. The grievance remains unresolved.

[3]This office had been the subject of an August, 1976 Arbitrator's Award, which directed the Department to improve conditions as soon as possible.

[4]Account of the situation taken from "Local 509 News," Vol. 9, Number 3, March 1977, pp. 1 and 4.

XII

MASSACHUSETTS DEPARTMENT OF PUBLIC WELFARE REPORT OF CHILD ALLEGED TO BE SUFFERING FROM SERIOUS PHYSICAL OR EMOTIONAL INJURY BY ABUSE OR NEGLECT

Please complete all sections of this form. If some data is unknown, please signify. If some data is uncertain, please place a question mark after the entry.

DATA ON CHILD REPORTED:

Name: _____

               Last   First   Middle

Address: _____

         Street & Number   City/Town   State

Sex: ☐ Male ☐ Female   Age: _____

DATA ON MALE GUARDIAN OR PARENT:

Name: _____

               Last   First   Middle

Address: _____

         Street & Number   City/Town   State

Telephone Number: _____   Age: _____

DATA ON FEMALE GUARDIAN OR PARENT:

Name: _____

               Last   First   Middle

Address: _____

         Street & Number   City/Town   State

Telephone Number: _____   Age: _____

Date of Report	Report received by telephone

Mandatory report/Voluntary report	Report received in writing

Name of Reporter: _____

               Last   First   Middle

Address of Reporter: _____

          Street & Number   City/Town   State

Telephone Number of Reporter: __   Relationship of Reporter to Child:

Name and Location of
Reporting Institution,
School or Facility: _____

   Street & Number   City/Town   State

   Telephone Number

CW-3C
1/75

What is the nature and extent of the injury, abuse, maltreatment or neglect, including prior evidence of same? (Please cite the source of this information if not observed first hand).

_____

_____

_____

_____

What are the circumstances under which the reporter became aware of the injuries, abuse, maltreatment or neglect?

_____

_____

_____

_____

What action has been taken thus far to treat, shelter or otherwise assist the child to deal with this situation?

_____

_____

_____

_____

Please give any other information which you think might be helpful in establishing the cause of the injury and/or the person responsible for it.

_____

_____

_____

_____

_____
Signature of Reporter (if written report)

===

DEPARTMENT USE ONLY

Time and date report received:

_____

Person receiving report:

| _____ | _____ | _____ |
| Name | Unit | Telephone |

Person assigned to investigate and evaluate situation:

| _____ | _____ | _____ | _____ |
| Name | Unit | Telephone | Assigned By |

===

XIII

Organization of the Case Folder

The case folder must be divided into six (6) sections. Each section must be clipped together in the upper left hand corner. The sections must be placed in the case folder from front to back in the following order:

— section 1: *Front Case Pocket* — a 5″ x 7″ manilla envelope stapled to the inside front cover of the case folder (POS 8, 8A's)

— section 2: *Face Sheet* in duplicate (see DF & CS Policy Statements Chapter IV p. 2 #1)

— section 3: *Family Record* "Blue Sheets" (see DF & CS Policy Statements Chapter IV-1 p. 2 #4 and see instructions for Pre-Formatted Recording Sheets)

— section 4: *Child Record* "White Sheets" (see DF & CS Policy Statements Chapter IV-1 p. 2 #4 and see instructions for Pre-Formatted Recording Sheets)

— section 5: *Correspondence;* filed in chronological order with the most current correspondence placed in the front of the section (see DF & CS Policy Statements Chapter IV-1 p. 2 #6)

— section 6: *Rear Case Pocket* — a 5″ x 7″ manilla envelope stapled to the inside back cover of the case folder. (See DF & CS Policy Statements Chapter IV-1 p. 2 #7)

In addition, for purposes of locating children and case folders two card systems must be maintained.

— Family Assignment Card (RSC-15) must be maintained for each family with a child in care and filed in a card file on the desk of the social worker.

— Supervision Card (CW 29) must be maintained, one card per child in care, and filed in a card file on the desk of the social worker

Forms and Materials to be Maintained
in the Case Record by Functional Areas

1. *General Intake/Assessment*
    a) Number Folder — one folder per family
    b) Intake Study — on "Blue Sheets" (See Existing Outlines, in Division of Family & Children's Policy Statements I-1)

c) CW 1 — Master Index Family Card — duplicate (one copy to Regional Office, one copy to Central Office)

d) RSC 15 — Family Assignment Card — one card per family. One copy for social worker, optional copies for supervisor or assistant director

e) CW 147 — Face Sheets — duplicate

f) SOC 1 — Request for Social Services

g) SOC 3 — Social Service Application

h) SOC 5 — Social Service Plan

i) SOC 7 — Information and Referral for Intradepartmental Interface (if appropriate)

j) SOC 9 — Information and Referral for an Interdepartmental or Community Resource Referral (if appropriate)

k) Front and Rear Case Pocket — 5" x 7" manilla envelope stapled to the inside front and rear covers of the case folder — all material placed in the pocket will be noted on front of pocket — (See DF & CS Policy Statements, Chapter IV-1 p. 2 #7)

l) POS 8 — Authorization for Services, placed in the front case pocket

m) Family Case Record "Blue Sheets" (See DF & CS Policy Statements, Chapter IV-1 p. 2 #6)

n) Correspondence Section — to begin with an identifying sheet (See DF & CS Policy and Procedures, Chapter IV-1 p. 2 #6)

o) CW 17A — Registration of an Oral or Written Report of Neglect or Abuse — (See Social Service Policy Manual Chapter II, Part 258.15, subpart C, p. 1 to be placed in pocket)

2. *Material to be Completed When Child Comes Into Care*

a) CW 2 — Master Index Child's Card — duplicate — (Copies to Regional and Central Offices)

b) CW 29 — Supervision Card — one card per child in care. One copy for Social Worker, optional copies for Supervisor and Assistant Director

c) Child's Record "White Sheets" (One set per child — see DF & CS Policy and Procedures Chapter IV-1 #4 and see instructions for preformatted case recording)

d) CW 7 — "23sA" to be signed by parent or guardian if child comes into care voluntarily (place in rear pocket)

e) CW 6 — "23E" — to be used if child is abandoned, signed by appropriate OSS supervisory personnel (place in rear pocket)

f) CW 7A — "23A" — to be used when child is born to a parent who is in prison (place in rear pocket)

g) CW 30 — Statement of Religion and Medical Care — to be signed by parent or guardian when they are available (place in rear pocket)

h) Mittimi or Petitions — sent to Department by court as a result of a court action under Chapter 119, Sections 25, 23D, 23C, 39G part C 39H (place in rear pocket)

i) CW 119 — Request for birth information (place in rear pocket)

j) CW 120 — Request for Verification of Marriage (place in rear pocket)

k) CW 120B — Request for Verification of Divorce (place in rear pocket)

l) CW 120C — Request for Verification of Death (place in rear pocket)

m) CW 4 — Certification of Birth Card (given to foster parents)

n) CW 31 — Medical Examination Report (see DF & CS Procedures & Policy)

o) CW 33 — Medical History

p) CW 17C — Notice of Removal of "reported Child" from usual place of residence — for Protective Service cases only 1/75.

q) POS 8 — Authorization for Services (place in front case pocket)

3. *Forms to be Used in Ongoing Cases*

a) CW 123 — "Section 23F" — a written agreement to keep in care a foster child who is above the age of 18

b) CW 31 — Medical Examination Report — continue to update in accordance with policy (see DF & CS Policy and Procedures Chapter IV-1 p. 2 #5)

c) CW 33 — Medical History

d) Mittimi, Petitions, Decrees, etc., resulting from court actions on the case

e) CW 154 — This form is filled out in duplicate when transmitting any case record material between Regional and/or local offices. The original accompanies the case record material that is being transmitted. The duplicate remains in the case files at the transmitting office. Place the CW 154 on the inside front cover of the folder. If entire case is transferred file all CW 154's in a separate file

f) R 52 — Application for a certified copy of a Birth Record (send to Vital Statistics, State House)

g) CW 122 — A worker request for an irregular payment to be made by the Bureau of Accounts to a foster parent or other provider for or on behalf of a child

h) POS 8A — Service Re-Authorization Form (Place in front pocket)

i) SOC 5A — Social Service Plan Reassessment Form

j) ADM 2 — Single Service Vendor Invoice, also used for back payment to foster parents

k) CW 17 B — Registration of results of Investigations and Evaluations of child alleged to be suffering from Abuse, Neglect or Addiction — See Social Service Policy Chapter II Part 258, Subpart J 258.104 Protective Service Cases only 1/75

l) CW 17D — Notice of Case Closing of "Reported Child" Notice to Central Protective Service Registry of the closing of a case presently listed in that registry — 1/75

4. *Group Care Referral*

a) A complete group care referral in accordance with existing outlines — copy to be placed in correspondence and noted in white sheets

b) CW 250 — Group Care Referral Card

c) CW 154 — When a child is actually placed in a group care facility a CW 154 should accompany material sent to G.C.U.

5. *Adoption Referral*

a) A complete adoption referral in accordance with existing outline

b) CW 130 — Referral Sheet sent to APU

c) CW 132 — Adoption Surrender — four copies — notarized — placed in rear pocket

d) CW 140A — Referral to Department Attorney requesting legal assistance to begin adoption actions

e) CW 140C — Form for filing of Adoption Petition

f) CW 140E — Notice to Social Worker by Department Attorney that Adoption Decree was granted

g) CW 140F — Notice from Adoption Worker to placement worker that an Adoptive home has been located

h) CW 143 — Notification to foster parent by Social Worker that child has been freed for adoption

6. *Material to be Continually Updated*

a) CW 1 — Master Index Family Card

b) CW 2 — Master Index Child Card

c) RSC 15 — Family Assignment Card

d) CW 147 — Face Sheet

e) SOC 5A's — Service Plan Reassessment

f) POS 8A's — Service Reauthorization

g) Child Record "White Sheets"

h) Family Record "Blue Sheets"

i) Correspondence Section

j) CW 29 — Supervision Card

k) CW 31 — Medical Examination Report

l) CW 33 — Medical History

m) CW 154 — Transfer Sheet

7. *Materials to be Placed in Front Pocket*

a) All copies of POS 8's and 8A's

8. *Materials to be Placed in Rear Pocket and Noted on Face of Pocket*

a) CW 3C — 51A report

b) CW 7 — "23sA"

c) CW 6 — "23E"

d) CW 7A — "23A"

e) CW 30 — Religion and Medical

f) All Mittimus's, court order, petitions, subpoenas, decrees, etc.

g) CW 119 — Request for birth information

h) CW 120 — Request for Verification of Marriage

i) CW 120B — Request for Verification of Divorce

j) CW 120C — Request for Verification of Death

k) CW 123 — Section 23F

l) Certified Copy of Birth

m) CW 132 — Adoption Surrender

n) CW 140 — Form for filing Adoption Petition

o) CW 140E — Notice to Social Worker of Adoption Decree

XIV

Group Care Unit — Child's Record Entry Worksheet

date:

CHILD: _____

PROGRAM: _____

(   )-(   ):
  date   GCU-SW

(   )-(   ):
  date   GCU-SW

(   )-(   ):
  date   GCU-SW

(   )-(   ):
  date   GCU-SW

XV

COMMONWEALTH OF MASSACHUSETTS
Department of Public Welfare

To: The Director of the Division of Child Guardianship
Department of Public Welfare

DATE: _____

I hereby request that you receive and provide foster care for_____

_____

_____

Under section 23, Subsection A of Chapter 119 of Massachusetts General Laws. In making this application, I also make a temporary delegation to the Department of the rights and responsibilities necessary to provide the foster care — including the determination of my child(ren)'s place of abode, medical care, and education. I agree to visit my child(ren) under conditions set up by the Department and agreeable to me. I am aware that this agreement may be terminated by me or by the Department with twenty-four hours' notice.

_____

Parent's Signature

_____

Address

_____

City and State

FINANCIAL AGREEMENT

I hereby agree to pay the Department of Public Welfare the sum of $_____
per week, payable_____ to reimburse in part the expense of
supporting my child(ren) _____

_____

_____

_____

Signature of Parent or Guardian

_____

Witness

Section 23, Subsection A of Chapter 119
of the Massachusetts General Laws:

Upon the application of a parent or guardian of any person acting in behalf of the
child, or of the child himself, the Department may accept for foster care any child
under twenty-one years who in its judgment is in need of foster care. Such
acceptance shall entail no abrogation of parental rights or responsibilities, but the
Department may accept from parents a temporary delegation of certain rights
and responsibilities necessary to provide the foster care for the period of time
under conditions agreed upon by both and terminable by either.

CW-7 Rev. 12-58
#2869